CW00952250

Camel Combat Ace

Dedicated to all British and Commonwealth airmen who flew and fought over the Western Front in World War One.

To my son Adrian with love and thanks for his constant support throughout a difficult year.

Camel Combat Ace

The Great War Flying Career
of Edwin Swale CBE OBE DFC[*]

Barry M. Marsden

Pen & Sword
AVIATION

First published in Great Britain in 2017 by
Pen & Sword Aviation
an imprint of
Pen & Sword Books Ltd
47 Church Street
Barnsley
South Yorkshire
S70 2AS

Copyright © Barry M Marsden 2017

ISBN 978 1 47386 684 3

The right of Barry M Marsden to be identified as the Author
of this Work has been asserted by him in accordance with the
Copyright, Designs and Patents Act 1988.

A CIP catalogue record for this book is available from the British
Library

All rights reserved. No part of this book may be reproduced or
transmitted in any form or by any means, electronic or mechanical
including photocopying, recording or by any information storage
and retrieval system, without permission from the Publisher in
writing.

Typeset in Ehrhardt by
Mac Style Ltd, Bridlington, East Yorkshire
Printed and bound in Malta by Gutenberg Press

Pen & Sword Books Ltd incorporates the imprints of Pen & Sword
Archaeology, Atlas, Aviation, Battleground, Discovery, Family
History, History, Maritime, Military, Naval, Politics, Railways,
Select, Transport, True Crime, and Fiction, Frontline Books, Leo
Cooper, Praetorian Press, Seaforth Publishing and Wharncliffe.

For a complete list of Pen & Sword titles please contact
PEN & SWORD BOOKS LIMITED
47 Church Street, Barnsley, South Yorkshire, S70 2AS, England
E-mail: enquiries@pen-and-sword.co.uk
Website: www.pen-and-sword.co.uk

Contents

Acknowledgements

In writing this book I must extend my grateful thanks to the late Margaret Howard, Edwin's daughter, her son Richard Rudin and her niece Helen Maley, whose interest and invaluable contributions have made this work possible. Sincere thanks also to Norman Franks for his invaluable help with 'planes and personnel.

Introduction

The Swales of Chesterfield, Derbyshire, were uniquely air-minded. Edwin Swale was a World War One fighter ace with seventeen victories, and his immediate family all took to the skies either in gliders or powered aeroplanes, or both. No fewer than three of the Chesterfield Swales were decorated with the Distinguished Flying Cross (plus a US DFC for good measure), and two of them gave their lives in successive Great Wars. Luckily Edwin's 1918 diary and logbook survive, as do those of his son Duncan who flew night intruder sorties over enemy territory in 1944–1945. Edwin also had a proud record as a councillor, alderman and mayor in his home town, and also served in the World War Two RAF, overseeing Ultra code-breaking intelligence with the 2nd Tactical Air Force.

I hope this narrative will do justice to the family's exemplary service in war and peace, and will stand as a tribute to the members who so graced my native township.

Barry M. Marsden
Eldwick, West Yorkshire

Chapter 1

Boyhood and Biplanes

Edwin Swale was a Victorian, born in Chesterfield in the June of the last year of the nineteenth century. His father, Arthur Whiteley Swale, listed as a 'tailor-cutter' in the 1901 census, came from Keighley in the Airedale-Wharfedale area of Yorkshire. In 1870, during a time of local depression in the woollen trade, Edwin's grandfather Seth brought his family to the north Derbyshire town where Arthur met and married a local girl, Emmeline Furness. Seth had opened a shop on Sheffield Road supplying clothes to people in the outlying mining villages of east Derbyshire. His three boys took the goods and samples by train, and the buyers paid for them in weekly instalments.

Arthur was somewhat of an entrepreneur who, in time, decided he would rather work for himself than for his parents and he was granted a mortgage from the Yorkshire Penny Bank to buy a property on Vicar Lane, near the town centre. He also 'yearned for respectability' according to a family member, perhaps concerned that his father, Seth, was an unusual personality for the time. As a committed atheist and socialist, described later by Edwin as a 'Marxist Atheist', he was perhaps not the ideal model for someone who wished to abide by the social *mores* of the day. The shop, selling clothes on the instalment scheme, and situated on a busy thoroughfare, prospered and quickly expanded by taking over the next-door premises.

An advertisement in *An Illustrated Guide to Chesterfield*, published in 1911, left readers in no doubt that the undertaking was on its way up. It read:

> Every article of men's, youths' or boys' outfit, from a necktie or a shirt to a suit of ready-made or measured clothing, is to be obtained of up-to-date quality at exceedingly moderate charges at this well-stocked establishment, where Mr. Arthur Swale is doing a large and increasing business in catering for these requirements of the local residents. The premises, situated in Vicar Lane, give every outward indication of the flourishing trade transacted, having the appearance of a first-class tailoring establishment, an aspect well borne out by the large and comprehensive stock of goods submitted for inspection in the window and the spacious interior. The principal features of the business are the well-cut and perfect-fitting garments supplied for every class of wear, the best material and excellent finish being assured, whether ready-made or bespoke.

Arthur's family, which included Edwin and his elder brother, Arthur Duncan, two years older than his sibling, moved to Tennyson Avenue, a smart, new, tree-lined thoroughfare full of local business and professional people with a certain community of interest. It is a singular fact when considering Edwin's career in the fledgling RAF that just across the street from the Swales lived the Bond family, whose eldest son, William Arthur, who trained as a newspaper reporter, volunteered for the army in 1914 and later became a Royal Flying

Corps 'ace' piloting Nieuport 17 scouts with 40 Squadron, winning the Military Cross and bar before his death in 1917. His wife, Aimee, told his story in her best-seller, *An Airman's Wife*, published in 1918. Bill's younger brother, Ernest, won the Military Medal as a gunner with the Royal Field Artillery, and was later awarded a commission with the South Staffords.

The Swales remained in Tennyson Avenue until 1913 when Arthur, by now somewhat wealthy, purchased Hady House, a fine Victorian property in rural surroundings on Hady Hill to the east of Chesterfield, with gardens on several levels, two coach houses and other extensive outbuildings. Edwin himself recorded that he enjoyed a happy childhood, strict according to the tenets of the age, but in a loving environment. His parents became members of the local Congregational Church and both children went to Sunday school and morning service as well. As they grew older they went to evening chapel, joined the Chapel Scout Troop and, in due course, Edwin became a committed Christian. The boys were educated at Chesterfield Grammar School, then a fee-paying establishment, and Edwin was certain his father made many sacrifices to give them a better start in life than he himself had enjoyed. He remembered that the family always took a fortnight's holiday each year, visiting such places as North Wales and the Isle of Man, and that when they entered their 'teens they were given bicycles, which enabled them to range locally across Derbyshire. The family also made occasional forays to stay with their relatives in West Yorkshire.

Edwin and Duncan did well at school, both educationally and at sports and games. The latter became School Captain, and the pair excelled at both cricket and football. Duncan was an accomplished wicketkeeper and full back, whilst Edwin, of lighter build than his brother, was a good batsman and a useful bowler, and both played in the school first teams. They also did well at athletics, Duncan winning the senior cup two years running, whilst his brother took the junior cup twice during the same period. Edwin later became skilled at tennis and golf, and also excelled at game shooting. His aptitude for sports, demanding instant reflexes, doubtless stood him in good stead for his later profession as a scout pilot, as they were essential attributes for a successful fighter and flyer. He also believed that his *alma mater*, as well as being of high academic standard, was also an excellent character-building establishment. He later wrote that the school made both brothers fit mentally and physically, 'and therefore able to play our part in the larger world into which we were dragged in such a violent way'. Edwin also learned to play the piano and organ, whilst Duncan mastered the violin, so well, in fact, that he became the second violinist in the town's local orchestra. On many Sunday evenings after chapel, the pair would play for whichever guests would be invited to supper.

Edwin recalled clearly the chapel service on 2 August, the Sunday evening before World War One began. The minister announced from the pulpit that Austria had invaded Serbia, and young Swale, then only 14, saw out of the west window of the building a blood-red sunset, and heard the minister's words, quoting the Foreign Secretary, that, 'Fires have been lit this day in Europe that this generation will never see extinguished.' The memory remained with him for the rest of his life. On the outbreak of war Duncan joined Nottingham University College in order to enter the Officer Training Corps and thus proceed into the army. He was duly commissioned into the local regiment, the Sherwood Foresters (the Nottinghamshire and Derbyshire Regiment). Eighteen months later, in January 1917, Edwin followed his brother into the University Officer Training Corps, remaining there until June of that year. He had determined on wartime service with the air force and applied to join the Royal Naval Air Service (RNAS).

At this time the army and navy ran their own air units, the latter the RNAS whilst the former were responsible for the Royal Flying Corps (RFC), though several squadrons of the RNAS operated under RFC command. For reasons he never made public Edwin decided to enlist with the RNAS, and was interviewed and medically examined at the Royal Navy's HQ at Admiralty Arch. He was accepted, but his call-up was deferred until he reached the age of 18. Within a day or two of his birthday he was requested to report to Greenwich Naval College in a probationary sub-lieutenant's uniform, which he had purchased in Derby. He found that he had been placed on a crash-course into the discipline, history, traditions and general routine of the Service before entering upon his flying training. He later reported that the cadets dined each night in some style in full uniform under the painted ceiling of the magnificent Great Hall of the establishment.

In early October Edwin was posted to the small airfield at Redcar in North Yorkshire for his *ab initio* flying training, which included navigation, the theory of flight, the workings of aero engines, and the design and construction of aeroplanes. His first flights were on a Farman Longhorn biplane, an archaic 'pusher' with the motor behind the pilot, the whole stately contraption being held together with bamboo struts and piano wire. He recorded that there were so many wires, 'that it was a joke of ours that if you took a bird with you into the cockpit and it could fly out and get away, there was a wire missing and you had better look out.' This very basic flying machine, in which instructor and pupil sat side-by-side, had controls:

> like a pair of spectacles, so that you could have both hands on it and it operated not only an elevator at the front but also one at the rear … there were two booms going back to the rear portion of the aircraft with its tail unit and rudder and the stick could move so that the aileron could be moved as well.

Edwin also noted that the machine was very stable and flew at a sedate speed, its air-cooled Renault V8 motor unable to cope with even moderate onshore winds. As the North Sea coast was nearby it was advisable not to let the contrivance drift offshore if a westerly was blowing. On one occasion Edwin did just that and was lucky to reach land again, after battling against a not-too-strong westerly breeze. In fact, he revealed that the Farman's speed could only be accurately judged by the noise of the wind whistling through the piano wires. He wrote, 'so you got a double sort of warning – if the whine was too high pitched you were going too fast.' Edwin was never happy when flying with an instructor, as it tended to make him nervous. Consequently, after only two hours' dual tutelage, which included one flight in an Avro 504 at Redcar, his instructor said he was ready to go solo but with the caveat, 'You can't land the bloody thing Swale, but if you'd like to take it up and break your bloody neck, you can go.' He went solo with his tutor's words ringing in his ears, and managed to complete the flight without damaging the machine or himself.

Edwin graduated from the Longhorn to the Avro 504, a more conventional aeroplane, 'in which you could do all the normal manoeuvres in comparative safety'. He always had a technical bent, and explained that this machine was powered by a French Gnome Rhone engine of rotary design in which the whole motor revolved around a stationary crankshaft. He explained that this power plant had one basic problem; the inlet valve which fed petrol into the cylinders depended on a spring-loaded valve in the piston head. The spring that returned each valve to its seating on the piston head had a tendency to weaken due to the heat generated by the motor, making it prone to breakage, thus jamming the inlet valve and initiating a stoppage, at, 'which point there was also a serious danger of fire'. If the engine 'conked' the unfortunate pilot had to hope he could glide down to a deadstick landing. Presumably, Swale managed to avoid this unscheduled end to any of his flights.

On the last day of 1917 Swale moved From Redcar, to the RNAS Central Flying School at Cranwell in Lincolnshire, a naval establishment that operated blimps that carried out anti-submarine patrols in the North Sea, as well as housing training aircraft. It was situated out in the countryside with comfortable accommodation and the base was where he felt his 'real education in flying took place'. Here he flew the BE2, the nippy little Bristol Scout and the equally delightful to fly Sopwith Pup. There were more lectures, practical sessions in the workshops, and cross-country navigating experience. On 18 February 1918 he moved on to Freiston near Boston for a gunnery and bombing course before a final spell at another naval station, Manston in Kent, from 23 February until 9 March, where he was brought up to date on the latest fighter formations and tactics, which he believed 'was one of the deciding factors which put the RAF in the position of dominating the skies before the end of the war'.

At Manston Edwin flew the Sopwith trio, the Pup, the Triplane and the Camel, the last being the up-to-date type he subsequently piloted during his time in France. Whilst based at the station he practised formation flying, later contrasting the orderly configurations used by the Royal Air Force with the 'bunched up masses' adopted by the German Air Service. He wrote that he strongly disagreed with the RAF ace James 'Ira' Jones who stated that, 'fighter formation flying didn't and wouldn't work. It did work and properly used we proved that it reduced our casualties and increased our kills.' He also noted that when operating over the battle front his squadron, consisting of 15 warplanes if all pilots were fit, were organized in three flights, A, B and C, with five aircraft to each flight, although Swale himself often favoured a three-plane 'vic'. Streamers on wing struts and tailfins picked out squadron and flight commanders, and hand signals helped to indicate aerial tactics. He was convinced that precise and disciplined formation tactics, properly used, worked well.

Even as an inexperienced flyer Edwin felt that fighter pilots, 'were God's chosen children. We reckoned we were a breed on our own and could make laws just to suit ourselves, and sometimes we did.' This arrogance was doubtless a good thing in shaping the outlook of airmen who were expected to be combative and who were infused with the offensive spirit of aggression and attack, carrying the air battle over the front lines and into enemy territory. On one occasion whilst at Manston he was taking part in a formation exercise with four other scouts, when he glimpsed an army remount unit practising with a group of horses that the troops were sedately riding. The quintet immediately side-slipped and came diving down, motors snarling, onto the hapless mounted outfit. The frantic equines began scattering in all directions at the noise, and the furious soldiery spent hours rounding them up from the miles of countryside they had galloped into in a frenzied effort to escape. The flyers managed to get away with the 'stunt', which was simply evidence of their daredevil spirit. He later wrote:

> If you didn't have a spirit like that you could not be a fighter pilot. You could call it high spirits, dare devil – call it what you like. We were full of life and spirit … even in the dark days when casualties were heavy and pilots were dropping every day, it was still maintained right to the very end.

Chapter 2

Above the Trenches

Naval flyers always crossed the Channel from Dover in destroyers to reach their units, and on 17 March Flight Sub-Lieutenant Edwin Swale made the passage to France. He was fortunate in meeting an old school friend on the pier, who was a signaller on duty. His friend promised, on conditions of the utmost secrecy, to write and tell Swale's parents that he was on his way to the front. He reported to the RNAS Reception Depot just outside Dunkirk, spending three days with No.12 Squadron RNAS, during which time he flew several of the unit's Camels, before a posting to No.10 at nearby Tetegham on the 23rd. No.10 Squadron had been formed in February 1917 and had been employed over the Western Front under the *aegis* of the RFC since May of that year.

No.10 Squadron flew the potent Sopwith Camel, successor to the Pup and Triplane. It was a little snub-nosed biplane and the first British fighter to carry twin .303in machine guns synchronized to fire through the airscrew disc. The scout aircraft, named after the hump above the engine cowling that housed the twin Vickers guns to prevent them freezing at altitude, could outmanoeuvre any contemporary enemy fighter but it needed expert handling, and the words fiery, temperamental and notorious have been applied to the skittish though formidable warplane. Because of the torque of its powerful rotary engine, the machine could turn very quickly to the right, an asset Camel pilots were quick to put to good use in combat. As one Canadian pilot put it:

> The Camel was one of the finest machines I ever flew, but when a young pilot initially went up in one he had to be awfully careful for the first 10 to 15 hours. Once he got through those he was safe.

Another pilot wrote, 'The Camel was so sensitive. You had to fly it all the time. When I got used to the aircraft it came easy, and it was wonderful in a dogfight.'

It is fortunate that Swale's flying logbook survives, plus a diary he kept throughout his time with his squadron. Though the entries in the latter were often brief, and provide few insights into his thoughts and feelings, the jottings help corroborate the more formal information from his log. Edwin also wrote an autobiography during his later years, which survives in typescript and helps to expand our understanding of the man for whom 1918 proved the defining period of his life. He had met Dorothy (Dolly) Asquith, by this time, through meeting her in chapel; she became his girl friend, fiancée and subsequently his wife, and his diary is infused with two consistent themes apart from his war duties – his longing for 'my Dolly' whom he missed and yearned for incessantly, and his obsession over mail, the delivery of letters, especially from Dolly, often making or breaking a particular day. Throughout the diary the twin subjects of Dolly and the post are mentioned practically on a daily basis, and form a constant, sometimes wearing, topic. The same preoccupation with mail is also evident in Aimee Bond's best seller *An Airman's Wife*.

Edwin's first operational flight was a 45-minute morning local familiarization in Bentley-powered Camel B3817 on the 23rd. 'Enjoyed myself immensely' was the comment in his diary. He was pleased with his new posting. 'The fellows are good,' he wrote, 'the quarters and food ditto and the weather as decent.' Though on the following day, in a bout of self-pity, he bemoaned the fact that not even the excitement of the Channel crossing 'stopped me thinking of Dolly, my Dolly and everyone at home'. On the afternoon of the 30th, Flight Sub-Lieutenant Maund took him on a 30-minute flight to view the lines between Nieuport, Dixmude and back to Dunkirk, localities he later got to know well from the air, though low-lying mist prevented him from seeing much of the ground on this occasion. On 1 April the RFC and the RNAS amalgamated to form the Royal Air Force, though this significant event escaped Edwin's diary. He was more concerned with his unit's move to Treizennes, south-east of St Omer, where the new quarters were 'moderately comfortable'. On that day No.10 became 210 Squadron RAF, all naval formations simply adding the number 200 to their original designation.

With the renumbering of 10 Squadron the rather flamboyant, not to say gaudy, RNAS paint scheme of the Camels, which consisted of black and white ('A' Flight), red and white ('B' Flight), and blue and white (C Flight) horizontally striped cowlings and forward fuselages, plus various coloured designs on the wheel discs, was gradually replaced by the more prosaic all-over dark green (not brown in 210's case according to Norman Wiltshire who personally examined two ex-210 Squadron Camels in a storeroom in Krakow Museum in Poland; he also checked out a piece of Camel centre-section kept by Swale and confirmed the dark green colouration), with dark-grey metal panels. The only subsequent concession to individuality was a white 'dumbbell' painted behind the fuselage roundel, whilst the flight letter, A, B or C was usually applied in front of the national marking.

Near the end of March the Germans, who had driven the Russians out of the war the previous year, launched their last great offensive in the West and Edwin was soon in action against the advancing field grey hordes. On the morning of 2 April he undertook his first operational patrol in B3940, crossing enemy lines for the first time and firing 100 rounds from his twin Vickers into La Bassée. It was his first experience of 'Archie', the often disconcertingly accurate German anti-aircraft fire, which was somewhat uncomfortable for the young rookie who was encountering the black airbursts for the first time. He confided to his diary that, 'Alex (Captain William Alexander, his Canadian flight leader) was pleased with my flying and it does me good to have praise from him more than I can say.'

On the following day an early morning patrol east of Lens in B3940 resulted in a further close peppering by enemy ack-ack, Edwin recording 'a big hole in my rudder' whilst other flight members suffered minor damage, including one whose goggles were 'smashed' by shrapnel. The Camels went down to strafe transport on the Arras–Cambrai road, the Derbyshire pilot rattling off 100 rounds from his Vickers from 1500 feet, suffering several return strikes from enemy bullets in the process. 'I guess we made it a bit warm for them,' was his laconic remark. Two blank days followed, due to poor weather, giving him time to visit Lillers, where he enjoyed tea, observing, 'It is a military town no doubt with it being close to Bethune.' On the 6th he was on solo pre-breakfast escort duty to an Airco DH4, the rest of his unit failing to find the reconnaissance aircraft due to the misty conditions. He protected his charge some three miles over enemy lines, and was later complimented by his CO, the Australian Major Bertram Charles Bell DSO DSC, whose brother Major Victor Douglas OBE also served with the RAF, commanding 80 Squadron in 1918.

Major Bell was an interesting character; a man of some means, he was visiting England when war broke out, and served for six months in France as an ambulance driver. In early 1915 he took private flying lessons and was commissioned a flight sub-lieutenant in the RNAS. He was posted to 1 Squadron RNAS in July and flew with them for eighteen months as a reconnaissance and light bomber pilot, before graduating to fighter duties on Nieuport 17s. He was awarded the Distinguished Service Cross in 1916 for 'conspicuous skill and gallantry'. In February 1917 he was posted to 3 Squadron RNAS, claiming seven victories whilst flying Sopwith Pups. He received the Distinguished Service Order for 'conspicuous gallantry and skill in attacking hostile aircraft' and from April of that year commanded 10 Squadron RNAS, holding the rank of major from April 1918 when the unit became part of the RAF. Edwin Swale later wrote that the major maintained his own private car and driver, and also kept a horse, both of which Swale drove or rode on occasion. Bell was later awarded the Belgian Croix de Guerre, but refused a permanent RAF commission after the war, returning to the Antipodes to farm. Sadly, he suffered a mental breakdown in 1941 and died shortly afterwards at the early age of 48.

Swale undertook several uneventful patrols during the following days, and on the 6th, whilst on a sweep with the whole squadron in his usual mount, he dived down too quickly from 18,000 feet and suffered a severe bout of air sickness. This left him feeling debilitated for the rest of the day, wishing, 'Dolly were here to be with me it wouldn't be half so bad then.' The following evening, he and Lieutenant Mellings dived on a series of barges moored on the La Bassée Canal, expending some 600 rounds from 1000 feet, and seeing men leaping from the boats into the water as the rounds impacted round them or raised plumes of spray around the vessels. Despite heavy machine gun fire neither aircraft was hit. 'There occurred a bit of panic,' he wrote later. 'Some sport but would rather have been in Chapel with Dolly'(!) Next day a teatime escort was aborted through mist, and the flight found it difficult to relocate their base. The flight commander Captain Alexander crashed his aircraft whilst attempting to land, but was, fortunately, unhurt. Edwin spent the evening at Aire, where he had dinner 'at the usual place'.

By 9 April the German advance had penetrated so far into the Allied lines that 210's airfield at Treizennes was in danger. When enemy shells began landing within 300 yards of the base the pilots were ordered to evacuate to Liettres, a few miles to the south-west. The pilots were ordered to help the ground staff to pack up all materials, load them onto all available transport and move everything to the new airfield. The pilots then returned to Treizennes to fly off their Camels. 'This we managed to do,' recalled Edwin, 'but we were actually taking off when one or two shells from German guns were bursting on the aerodrome.' They were to operate from this new 'aerodrome' (in the phraseology of the time) on a permanent basis. According to Edwin the living quarters 'were heaps better than the old ones'.

On the 10th, 210's Camels, which had been fitted with underwing racks for light 20lb Cooper anti-personnel bombs, carried out their first ground-attack missions. The bombs, originally four, but later reduced to two, were released by a Heath-Robinson arrangement consisting of a length of wire that came through the cockpit floor close by the pilot's right hand. Affixed to the wire was a toggle, which was activated by a smart tug, each tug hopefully releasing one missile. There was no aiming device of any kind, the pilot simply flying at some 500 feet in the vicinity of his target and trusting to luck that the bombs would disengage. The only indication that they had released was a sudden lightness on the controls. The devices were highly unpopular with the flyers as sometimes they failed to leave the racks, with the danger that they might fall off and explode on landing. Nevertheless, for some weeks Edwin was occupied with dropping his loads on any suitable targets, the overburdened scouts staggering into the air with 80lb of excess weight to contend with, and which restricted the Camels' ceiling to 3000 feet.

Swale dropped his first quota of bombs against ground targets on the 10th, following up with trench strafing runs during which he aimed 400 rounds at enemy troops. He got lost in ground mist on return to base, but eventually landed safely, noting he was now settled in the new quarters. On the 11th he carried out two trench strafes in a new machine, B3817, getting rid of his four bombs, and engaging the German Air Force for the first time. His antagonist was a two-seater, type not specified, but as he closed with his quarry, an enemy scout came at him from above and behind, firing a fortunately inaccurate burst before diving past the Derbyshire aeronaut, who quickly sought shelter in a convenient cloud. In worsening weather he found himself lost and attempted to land in a field near Hazelbrouck.

Edwin's flying time with B3817 was sadly brief, as he stalled the Camel as he turned in to alight, the machine spinning in with the nose hitting a ditch and the wings breaking the force of the impact with a splintering crash. He recorded that he had 'smashed the machine altogether' and was 'lucky to escape with a few scratches', which included grazing his face on one of the gun butts. He managed to contact a nearby Army Remount Depot whose field telephone enabled him to contact his base who told him to stay with his aeroplane until it could be rescued by trailer from the advancing enemy.

What Edwin Swale endured over the next few hours stayed with him for the rest of his life as, whilst he awaited assistance, he had a taste of what war meant to the local civilian population. Hundreds of French refugees, men, women and children, escaping *en masse* from the advancing 'Huns', came streaming past him on a nearby road, anxious only to escape the oncoming foe. As he wrote in his autobiography:

> I saw hundreds upon hundreds of families struggling with all the possessions they had left in the world. Old prams were being pushed with household goods stacked on them, the men and women had packs on their backs – screaming children, tired women – and I could see the whole futility from a civilian point of view as to how war affected the ordinary men and women who were involved in the actual fighting area. This was one of the sights which brought home to me what war really did mean and which I had never experienced until that actual time.

'Some night,' he confided to his diary as he staggered home to his quarters, doubtless worn out, at 4 a.m.

The following afternoon he was back in business piloting his usual mount, B3940. He released his four Coopers over Merville, being rewarded with the outbreak of a large fire and followed up with a strafing run against German troops in the open, loosing off some 400 rounds and confessing he had peppered the unfortunate soldiery 'pretty thoroughly'. He also commented on his subsequent good landing at base 'after my smash of yesterday'. On the 14th, again piloting B3940 on a late afternoon sortie, he released his bomb load on enemy supply vehicles east of Merville and followed up by attacking transport on the Merville–Estaires road, loosing off over 500 rounds. On a back road behind the German lines, he picked out a staff car containing several officers which he pursued until the panicking driver ran off the road and overturned the motor into a ditch, spilling its occupants in the process. Swale enjoyed, 'a hearty good laugh. This was great fun.'

The next day, on an early morning mission, in a field south-east of Merville, Edwin spotted a German Remount Depot, with dozens of horses lined-up and tethered alongside a hedge. He realized that this was a vital target as German supply and artillery transport was largely horse-drawn. He dropped his bombs alongside the field housing the animals, and followed up by running his Camel above the lines of horses, with both guns blazing. The panicked beasts broke their ropes and scattered wildly across the countryside in a terrified stampede, doubtless causing huge confusion to the enemy and, as Swale realized, helping in some small way to hinder their advance.

April the 16th was a washout through bad weather, Edwin visiting Estrée Blanche for an afternoon stroll. In the evening he wrote, 'By the sound of the guns the Huns are attacking again. We shall look well if we have to leave the Drome.' Next day an early morning mission saw him bombing and strafing German front-line trenches in B3940. One of his bombs scored a direct hit on the target, whilst he rattled off 150 rounds to keep the enemies' heads down. In a later patrol in poor visibility he lost his way and landed near Boulogne, slightly damaging his Camel as it became entangled in a wire fence on sloping ground. He was forced to spend the night at No.12 Convalescent Camp, in the Officers' Mess. Next day he supervised the packing-up of his unfortunate B3940 and did not get back to base until 7 p.m. His diary recalled that, 'It was some job to get the machine packed and pulled up the hill side.'

On the 19th, wind and hail storms restricted flying, and Edwin took the opportunity to visit St Omer that evening, reporting that he enjoyed 'a nice quiet time'. He strolled through the park and, in a reflective moment, looked over the Notre-Dame Catholic Church, 'which is beautiful beyond description'. The next day, a dawn patrol in B6358 saw him deposit four bombs on La Bassée in the face of heavy flak. That evening, reunited with his faithful B3940, he glimpsed three Fokker DR1 Triplanes above his formation, but, in the face of an aggressive climb by the Camels, the enemy warplanes swung away and disappeared. The following afternoon his flight picked out enemy aircraft below them on an offensive patrol over Merville, but their ensuing dive was aborted as further German scouts appeared above them. Swale recorded, 'Very little AA which is strange after having so much lately.' That evening he enjoyed a stroll with Lieutenant Baird, but 'would much rather have been at Church with Dolly and Mother and Dad'. On the 25th a late morning 'stunt' over La Bassée-Merville produced no Huns but 'plenty of Archie which was too jolly close to be pleasant'.

On the 26th, after a few days of poor weather, the squadron received orders to move from Liettres to St Omer to the north. Edwin was not impressed, noting that 'the quarters are rotten when compared to Liettres'. They took up occupation on the following day and two afternoons later the Derbyshire aviator was again busy bombing Merville. South of much-battered Ypres he picked out two Albatros V Scouts, firing an ineffective burst at one. Shortly afterwards he dived on two more enemy fighters west of Bailleul, aiming 100 rounds with no apparent effect. On an afternoon of low cloud he patrolled the Bailleul–Ypres area and had his first look at the much battered locality. 'Had my first real look at Ypres,' he confided to his diary – 'poor city.' The following day he had to take sharp evasive action when a flight of Camels mistook him for an enemy, and on 3 May, whilst landing his ever faithful B3940 after a sortie patrolling Ypres–Nieppe Forest, he broke his axle. He was airborne again at 3.10 p.m. in B6242 between Bailleul and Ypres, but stayed aloft too long, and can't have been the most popular aeronaut in the unit, when he ran out of petrol, as he landed and careered across the airfield, crashing into four parked Camels, damaging each of the quartet as he hit them in turn. 'I am beginning to get used to crashes,' was his laconic comment.

The following morning, with B3940 again airworthy, Edwin loosed four bombs over Bailleul, but turned back on a later mission with unspecified engine trouble. The 5th was a day of heavy sheeting rain with 'one of the heaviest thunderstorms I have experienced', whilst on the 6th hc was patrolling just west of Ypres when a rocker arm broke at 16,000 feet, necessitating a second premature return to base. On the 7th he wrote, 'The Gun Fire tonight is Getting terrible, either we are attacking or the enemy is' whilst next day he had to return early from a sweep in B3940 with a further broken rocker arm. He carried out a second patrol in B6242 before reclaiming his usual mount, and shortly after 10 a.m. he was patrolling the Armentières–Ypres line when he saw twelve enemy scouts below him. He promptly dived on one, aiming a short burst without effect, before transferring his attention to a second warplane, snapping off fifty rounds. As he broke away after his attack one of his landing wires parted and he was forced to return home. He must have received an unpleasant shock as an enemy fighter came up alongside him as he headed for base, but the Hun, perhaps out of ammunition or low on fuel 'didn't attack and it was a good job for me he didn't'.

Later that day he loosed off a quick burst at an enemy two-seater near Bethune, and the next morning, near Armentières, he dived on three Albatros aircraft, firing a long but ineffective burst at one as they disappeared rapidly eastwards, outpacing his slower Camel. A German two-seater put in an appearance, and Swale engaged this, pumping 50 rounds into the aeroplane with no apparent results. By this time Edwin must have been wondering if he was ever going to nail an enemy warplane. That evening he released four bombs over Coumines and reported that, 'Archie was too close to be pleasant tonight.' On the 10th, poor weather prevented any air operations, and he took the opportunity to test two newly installed Vickers guns on his new mount, D3392, on the squadron range.

On the early afternoon of 11 May, west of Merville in D3392, Swale lined up an enemy two-seater, doubtless believing his first kill was about to be marked up. To his chagrin both machine guns spat out ten rounds before jamming, and he veered away in frustration. It was difficult to clear stoppages whilst flying, and was certainly not recommended during combat! At 6.20 p.m. his Coopers, four out of 92 released over Armentières by several Camel units, produced 'good results' including an ammunition dump set ablaze, after which the squadron became involved in a dogfight with some twenty German scouts in which 210 claimed one 'flamer' and two out-of-control. Sadly, Swale saw a Camel of 4 Australian Flying Corps going down on fire. 'It was an awful sight,' he commented as the blazing machine plummeted to earth. On their return their Camels became lost in thick ground mist that had suddenly appeared and pancaked at Oudezeele, north of Cassel. Edwin landed safely, though several other pilots and aircraft suffered damage as they came down in the murk. Two squadron pilots, Arnold and d'Etchegoyan were badly injured in the landings, with the latter dying in hospital on the 13th. 'What a time' he recorded of the experience. 'Frost in hospital … Carter cut his lip badly. I hope I never have to go through it again,' he continued, 'or my nerves will go.' The following day he flew his machine back to St Omer despite strong winds, trusting, 'I have got into the CO's good books again through this little lot.' Presumably his little effort on 3 May was still on his mind.

On the 13th bad weather kept the unit grounded, giving Edwin the opportunity to visit St Omer for tea and a much needed bath, but the next day, after fetching a new Camel, D3387, from No.1 Air Supply Depot, he was aloft on an evening sortie in B3392, releasing four Coopers on much-hit Armentières. North of ruined Ypres he dived on five enemy scouts, but his single burst produced no apparent effect. Armentières was subjected to further bombing the following morning, but later that day Edwin recorded the deaths of two squadron comrades, Lieutenants Hall and Kelly, who collided over the lines 'with little hope for either'. That afternoon he attacked five Pfalz DIII scouts over Armentières without effect.

Early on the 16th near Ypres, Swale dived on an enemy two-seater, loosing off fifty rounds from only 100 yards range, but still failing to record any damage, a result that must have been disheartening to say the least. Later on he was attacked by a Fokker Triplane as his whole patrol were intercepted by a mixed bunch of enemy scouts. His machine, B3392, must have been hard-hit by enemy fire, though his comments on the incident were laconic to say the least, as on return to base it required a new centre-section and bottom plane. Edwin seems to have enjoyed a lucky escape. Next morning, piloting replacement Camel D3390, he was attacked by eight Pfalz and Albatros DV hostiles over Merville who chased him back over the lines. As he re-crossed the trenches he was assailed by five more German fighters, which he evaded without damage.

On the late morning of the 18th, flying his familiar B3940. he loosed off some 600 rounds at an enemy DFW CV reconnaissance two-seater at long range east of Armentières, but could not close the range sufficiently to ensure any hits. He recorded in his diary that two of 210's pilots, Lieutenants Hollick and Sutton, were missing from an evening mission, whilst during the night the unit's base was subjected to a bout of bombing. 'Big Air raid tonight' he recorded. 'Ammunition dump and train blown up. Don't like bombs at all.' He confessed, 'It is the worst experience I have had so far.' He might in future have had some sympathy for the enemy troops who had been subjected to his own frequent missiles! On the next day, patrolling over Bailleul–Mount Kemmel in D3381, he picked out another DFW two-seater north of the town. He expended 300 rounds from his twin Vickers and succeeded in driving the intruder away despite seeing no definite results from his fire.

On 21 May, flying in D3392, Swale was part of a mid-morning escort to three British fighters attacking German observation balloons near Armentières, seeing four of the targets going up in flames, followed by a similar afternoon sortie during which a further inflatable was set on fire. On the following day he again bombed much-abused Armentières before attacking a pair of two-seaters east of Kemmel. The enemy warplanes immediately turned on him and drove him back over his own lines. 'They gave me a warm time of it,' he confessed. Early on the 23rd Neuf Bequir was the new target for his four Coopers, but an attack on four enemy scouts was thwarted when they dived away, speedily outdistancing his own aircraft. He spent the afternoon in St Omer, where he had tea, but was unable to get a bath. Dolly and home were much in his thoughts at this time, and he wrote of his 'wanting her so'.

On the 24th, poor weather put off air operations but the squadron was inspected by Major General Herbert Plumer, later viscount and field marshal. 'The usual thing happened,' recorded a cynical Swale. 'He said lots of nice things about us.' Edwin followed the visitation by the usual tea in St Omer, which made 'quite a nice change'. Over the next two days, by now flying D3392 as his personal machine, Edwin dropped his bombs on Bac St Maur; on the latter day 210 acted as escort to a balloon strafe, whilst on the late afternoon of the 27th he experienced a tricky end to a mission when his bombs hung up on their racks and failed to drop. He brought off a successful if nerve-racking landing without mishap, and the offending missiles were speedily removed. Remarkably, though his log recorded the event, his diary preserved complete silence, reporting that 'nothing particular happened'!

Swale enjoyed some target practice on the Clairmarius range on the 28th, whilst on the 29th heavy clouds blew up on an early morning patrol, forcing him and fellow airman Lieutenant Baird to land at Alquines airfield, fifteen miles west of St Omer and home to 206 Bomber Squadron. They returned home by 9.15 a.m. and by 6 p.m. he was busy dropping ordnance over Bac St Maur, followed by a vain chase after enemy scouts fleeing over Nieppe Forest. By this time, after almost two months of operational duty and shooting vainly at a series of opponents, Edwin must have been wondering if a hostile warplane would ever fall to his guns. However, this was all to change on the morning of Thursday 30 May.

After depositing two bombs on Bac St Maur, Swale's unit met with five Pfalz D111 scouts at 17,000 feet, west of Armentières at 11.30 a.m. Piloting his familiar D3392, he came down behind an all-green enemy fighter, lining up the angular biplane in his gunsight. A dose of 100 rounds from his twin Vickers produced no results, so he pulled away and repeated his attack, following his diving quarry down to 8000 feet and firing several bursts at very close range. Repeatedly hit by his tracers, the hapless Pfalz fluttered down completely out-of-control and crashed on the bank of the canal just west of the town. 'Got my first Hun!' he confided to his diary. 'Am coming on'! He must have been heartily glad to have at last broken his duck. The next day he was able to confirm his kill, seeing the broken wreckage of the shot-down scout on the canal bank as he flew overhead.

The 30th was a hectic day in all respects as the unit received orders to redeploy to an airfield at St Marie Cappel, east of St Omer, later that day. 'Quarters champion,' was Edwin's verdict, 'but Drome rotten beyond description. I guess there's going to be some crashes here.' Swale was soon in action from his new home. Up on the Dawn Patrol at 3 a.m. on the 31st, near the Nieppe Forest his flight spied a gaggle of Pfalz and Albatros scouts below, and he was soon dogfighting with one of the latter. The pair circled, descending as low as 5000 feet, at which point he broke off the engagement. Later that morning he unloaded four bombs on much-hit Bac St Maur and drove off an enemy two-seater away from the totally devastated Nieppe Forest where the German advance had finally been halted in Swale's sector of the line. Further comments on his new headquarters were confided to his diary. 'The Drome is simply awful here,' he wrote. 'I haven't made a decent landing on it yet.'

The unfortunate Bac St Maur was subjected to two Swale attacks on the first day of June, and that evening he visited a nearby British kite balloon base, where he saw one of the giant inflatables being winched aloft. 'It was jolly interesting,' was his somewhat vague though enthusiastic comment. A patrol with Bristol F2B Fighters on the 2nd saw D3392 hit in the fuselage by German ack-ack, whilst the following two days were spent in preparation for a 'balloon strafe', which was postponed twice due to unfavourable weather. On the 3rd Captain Ray Hinchliffe, flying back a forced-down Camel, crashed in a cornfield whilst landing in the dark. He suffered severe facial injuries and lost his left eye. He wore an eye patch for the rest of his life, and post-war flew with both the Dutch KLM and Imperial Airways, racking up over 9000 flying hours. He disappeared, together with Elsie Mackay, millionairess daughter of Lord Inchcape, whilst attempting an east-west crossing of the Atlantic in March 1928. His life has been the subject of a book and film, both entitled *The Ghost of Flight 401*.

The balloon attack eventually took place on the 5th at 10 a.m., when the flight was escorted by Bristol F2Bs. Anti-balloon operations were considered the most dangerous of all 'stunts', the aerial equivalent of 'going over the top' as the observation blimps were invariably well protected by fighters and surrounded by plentiful AA positions. Six of the inflatables were strung out at 3000 feet east of Estaires and 210's Camels plunged through an intense flak barrage to reach them. Edwin closed to within twenty yards of his target, seeing his tracer score around one hundred hits as the huge gasbag sagged away in flames, a victory confirmed by fellow pilot Lieutenant 'Bert' Jones. Swale witnessed the German observers swiftly leaping from their underslung baskets and taking to their parachutes as Nemesis approached. Apart from his own 'kill' another balloon was set on fire, and two more deflated and went down wreathed in smoke. Edwin wrote, 'they gave us hell with machine guns and Archie,' and though D3392 was hit in the engine, he was able to return safely. Incidentally, fellow pilot Albert Leslie Jones was one of the characters of the unit. On one occasion he incurred his CO's ire by blazing away at some inoffensive sparrows with his service revolver. Major Bell concluded he was too irresponsible to own the weapon and had it confiscated. Nevertheless, the eccentric young man, who was witness to Edwin's successful attack, recorded seven victories with the squadron, despite suffering bouts of air sickness, before he was deemed ready for a rest from operations, and was posted to Home Establishment on 13 August.

On the 7th Swale reported two 'stunts' during which, 'The Archie was something awful and I got the wind up vertically.' He had a right to do so as his aeroplane was hit in the lower planes by bursting shrapnel, an event repeated the following evening when the long-suffering D3392 was again peppered. 'The Archie round here is getting unpleasant,' he noted. 'Somebody is going to be hit if we aren't very careful. I got another chunk in one of my ailerons again today.' Early on the 9th, after further bombs on Bac St Maur, Lieutenant Marsden, flying immediately behind Edwin, was shot down by a Triplane, possibly a machine from *Jasta* 30, and one other pilot, Lieutenant Breckenridge, was missing after the mission. The next day was another tragic one for 210's airmen when, flying home in a heavy rainstorm, two pilots, Captain Mansell and Lieutenant Dodd, collided over the front line, 'with no hope for either'. 'What luck this squadron has,' he wrote in reflective vein. 'Whose turn next I wonder?'

The bad luck continued on the 11th when Lieutenant Mason was killed in a flying accident on the airfield, whilst Swale complained that he had been 'transferred to B Flight, worse luck', though he did not reveal the reason for his grievance. He probably did not remain long there as he eventually took over 'A' Flight at the end of August. Poor visibility hindered operations for the next two days, though bombing continued, and he fetched a new machine, D9613, from the depot, which was to be his own personal scout, on the 12th. There was some time for leisure, as on that same day the officers played the other ranks at cricket, 'but lost hopelessly'. He flew his new mount on the 13th, loosing two Coopers over his favourite target, Bac St Maur, and next day tested his guns on the range at Clairmarius but to his chagrin both his Vickers suffered stoppages. This was followed by a leisurely afternoon in St Omer, for a hot bath and tea, which included strawberries and cream, evidently somewhat of a treat to merit mention in his diary!

The much-battered Bac St Maur, against which Swale seems to have harboured a personal grudge, was assaulted on six successive days, from 15 to 20 June. On the former date he intercepted a two-seater east of Merville, but his pressure system failed and he was unable to open fire on his quarry. German aerial activity had tailed off in mid-month and he enquired of his diary, 'What has become of them? The calm before the storm I expect.' However, on the 17th, on an early morning sortie on the Ypres–Merville–Lille line, after the usual bombs on Bac St Maur, his patrol glimpsed a mixed gaggle of eight Fokker and Albatros scouts at 10,000 feet south-east of Zillebeke Lake. His flight leader, Captain Herbert Patey, attacked an Albatros DV biplane, and Swale, following behind, hammered fifty rounds into the same machine from the point-blank range of twenty-five down to fifteen yards. The German fighter spun down out of control, with Edwin pursuing it down to 6000 feet. The stricken warplane crashed south-east of the lake, a demise confirmed by Captain Patey, an AA battery and a pilot of 20 Squadron. Another enemy aircraft, presumably hit by fire from several 210 pilots, was also despatched, 'which goes to the credit of the Flight'. Unhappily, Lieutenant Campbell was killed in the affray, and Lieutenant Strickland wounded. Edwin wrote that Patey had gone on leave that evening instead of him, 'due to circumstances' but that he had only another week to wait before he too was due for a rest. Bad luck continued to haunt the unit on the 18th when Lieutenant Shackell died in a flying accident near the base. 'The rotten luck of the Squadron seems to be holding still,' he wrote. 'It's awful.'

On the 20th an afternoon flight in D9613 was aborted due to engine trouble, whilst on the 19th, a day of poor visibility, he witnessed a German fighter, apparently intent on attacking British observation balloons, being brought down by 29 Squadron's SE5a aircraft. 'It was some scrap,' he wrote, 'and we saw it all from the Drome.' On the 21st the unit relaxed with a cricket match between the pilots and ground crew. The latter scored 88 – heaven knows on what sort of wicket – and Edwin not only took five wickets for 28 runs, but scored 28 in the flyer's reply of 49 for 2. Two of his bombs on Estaires on the 23rd started a large fire, and for the first time he led a flight of three Camels, engaged in an evening sweep when two enemy fighters were shot down.

On the early morning of 24 June, in a search for a reconnaissance two-seater over Nieppe, Swale's flight dived through clouds and he found the enemy aeroplane directly beneath him. The wide-awake Hun turned quickly under the RAF fighters and escaped into the murk before the frustrated flyers of 210 could nail him. 'I had hard luck with Old Man Hun' were the thoughts Edwin committed to his diary, which also recorded that another squadron aviator, Lieutenant Fearn, had been shot down near Zillebeke later that morning. That afternoon he was put in charge of a group of new officers who toured several French and American bases 'to see Breguets and Spads'. 'Had quite a nice time,' he confided, 'only it was tiring.' He relaxed by stopping off at Berques for tea. The next day he reported seeing 'Flaming Archie' for the first time whilst on a bombing sortie to the battered Bauc St Mair.

The 26th was Edwin's last day on the squadron before his leave commenced. He celebrated it by bombing Lille and witnessed two enemy two-seaters being despatched in flames by his unit, 'but poor old Boothman is missing'. On the 27th he began a well-deserved fortnight's rest, with some 240 hours' solo flying in his log, plus some six hours dual. His leave train was three hours late, he reached Boulogne in the early hours of the 28th, his nineteenth birthday, and was home in Chesterfield by 9.10 p.m. the following evening. His diary entry recorded, 'Oh what a lovely home-coming. The only thing that mars it is the thought of going away again, but sufficient unto the day.'

Chapter 3

Camel Ace

Edwin Swale's leave, the only one he enjoyed in over six months' active service, was an idyllic one; on Sunday 30 June his diary recorded that he had proposed to his sweetheart Dolly and had been accepted. 'Oh what perfect joy', he gushed romantically, 'to be able to claim her as my own.' Lower down on the page he wrote 'My Red Letter Day' with 16/12/18 enclosed in a rectangle. Presumably this was meant to be his wedding day. If so, unforeseen circumstances prevented the nuptials from happening until much later. Little else was committed to the pages of his diary during the fortnight, apart from several unspecified but 'lovely' days, with a visit to the 'pictures' described as being 'quite like old times'.

Edwin left home for France at 11.56 p.m. on the 11 July, remarking, 'The Parting was awful. I can't say anything else.' Though he did later reflect, 'It was not so easy to go back and yet I did go back in a better mental state than I had before.' He reached Boulogne at 2 p.m. the following day, and arrived at St Omer at 8 p.m. that night, finding that the unit had redeployed to Tetegham three days earlier. He wrote that, 'We are now attached Navy and it seems better.' Indeed, another squadron member had indicated that 'some of our duties in future will be carried out in conjunction with the Royal Navy', including coastal patrols and suchlike. The change involved a move from 22 Wing, 5 Brigade, their former placement, to 61 Wing, 5 Group.

Edwin arrived back with 210 a seasoned and professional pilot; during the next few months he proved his worth by rapidly increasing his own personal score and ending up as a flight leader. However, his return was anything but orderly as he reached Tetegham late at night with his gear unpacked and nowhere to rest. He borrowed a sleeping bag, found a berth and was later scheduled for an afternoon patrol in D9613 with his flying gear mislaid. He eventually led his flight in ordinary clothes and a borrowed flying helmet after two nights without much sleep. 'This was the sort of hectic life we led,' he commented later. Little wonder that on his first mission, a 4.20 p.m. prowl over Ostend-Nieuport, 'I couldn't keep formation for nuts' and 'had to turn back eventually owing to landing wire breaking'.

Things did not improve on the following day. Again piloting D9613 on a morning mission, his motor 'conked' two miles east of Ypres and he was forced into a hasty deadstick landing at Proven airfield, north-west of Poperinge, where he amused himself whilst a new engine was installed in his machine. He 'had a good time there' before returning to base at 8 p.m. On the 16th he again led a flight of three Camels escorting Airco DH9 bombers to the far side of Zeebrugge, no easy task as the fast light bombers took some keeping up with. Next day he was again home early with engine trouble, and after two days of indifferent weather, during which he recorded 'some of the finest lightning I have seen' he undertook two coast patrols as part of 210's naval duties, searching fruitlessly for enemy seaplanes, the first as a result of a report by the Kentish Knock Lightship. During the second quest the Camels scouted some thirty miles out to sea and as far north as Ostend, no happy experience in a single-engined biplane.

A new idea was tried out on the morning of the 20th when the squadron made a long right hook via Ypres, Roulers (modern Roeselare), Bruges and Blankenberghe to Ostend, where some fifteen Fokker biplanes were encountered at 18–19,000 feet south-east of the port. The foes were DVIIs, dangerous new adversaries only recently introduced into the German *Jastas*. Edwin squeezed off some 100 rounds into one of his opponents at thirty yards' distance and saw it go down streaming grey smoke as it fell away out of control. Destruction was subsequently confirmed by Captain Mellings. There was no time for congratulation as another Fokker came down on his tail and, using the Camel's speedy right-hand turn, Swale swung tightly under his adversary, attacking it from astern and hitting it with a 100-round burst at sixty yards. The warplane turned lazily over on its back and went tumbling down from the sky. Back at base confirmation was given for two victims both claimed downed. One of his victims may have been FlugzgMstr Alfons Nitsche of *Marine Feld Jasta* 11, reported crashed and killed at Leffinge. After the morning's thrills Edwin laconically announced that he 'went into Dunkirk in the afternoon'.

On 22 July, 210 made its final move of the war, relocating to Eringhem, a few miles south of Dunkirk. That same afternoon, on an offensive patrol over Ostend at 16,000 feet, seven Fokker DVIIs were seen below. Swale dived on one of the enemy biplanes, expending some 100 rounds at eighty yards and seeing his tracers hit home. The stricken Fokker turned slowly on its back and plummeted down in an almost vertical dive. The Derbyshire flyer could not observe its end as he was attacked by a second enemy warplane, which he shook off by another violent turn. Confirmation of the kill was given by Lieutenant Sutcliffe. It was Swale's fourth victim, plus the one balloon, which gave him the coveted status of an ace. Sadly, his diary recorded that two of his comrades were missing by the end of the day, Lieutenant Bullen, an American attached to the squadron, and the redoubtable Captain Harold Mellings DSC and bar, DFC, killed in action with Jasta 56 after claiming two victories earlier that same day. He was only 18 and is buried in Ramscappelle Road Military Cemetery, Nieuwpoort, Belgium. On an early morning patrol two days later severe enemy ack-ack exploded among the flight, scattering the Camels and hitting D9643 in the elevator. He subsequently recorded that we 'got more than we wanted in the way of Archie'. His brother was on leave at the time and Edwin expressed his heartfelt wish that 'I could be home now to see Duncan.'

Bad weather hampered aerial operations for much of the rest of the month. Edwin must have had some difficulties with an errant batman whom he had to 'run in to the CO' with undisclosed results, on the 25th. On the 29th, one squadron pilot, Lieutenant Jenkins, crashed into the sea in the hazy conditions after taking part in an eleven-plane offshore patrol, but was fortunate to be picked up by a paddle steamer shortly afterwards, a drama witnessed by Swale himself. Later that evening three pilots managed to crash their mounts whilst landing, again in poor visibility, but fortunately without any serious injuries. After two indecisive combats on the 30th, Edwin's luck held on the following morning when eight enemy warplanes dived on his formation, which was badly split up. He heard the dreaded crackle of Spandau machine guns as two German scouts pursued him, but Captain Patey, despite being hit in the petrol tank and suffering from a misfiring engine, shot one of the Fokkers off his companion's tail, which crashed into a flooded area just north of Dixmude, whilst the other prudently took to his heels.

On 1 August, piloting D9675, Edwin led a vic of three on a fruitless morning on the Roulers-Ostend line, but that evening his formation picked out some fifteen German scouts north of Lille at 16,000 feet. Edwin lined up a Fokker DVII gaily camouflaged in green and yellow. He put in a seventy-round burst at some fifty yards' range and the hard-hit aircraft went down in a flat spin on its back and 'absolutely out of control' a demise later confirmed by Captain Patey. A general melee ensued before the enemy broke off the action, and 210's claims totalled six hostile aircraft. Major Bell was so pleased with the unit's 'recent activities' that, 'he said we could have transport tomorrow to St Omer to celebrate our successes.'

There was little combat for the remaining first few days of the month, though on the 4th Edwin wrote there could have been some evening action, 'as there were plenty of Huns around but as Chambers and I were by ourselves we couldn't take on the whole German Air Service'. Things were enlivened by a visit from 201 Camel Squadron from St Marie Cappel on the 5th, which ensured a spirited evening in the mess, with much conviviality. There was 'a full out night at the Squadron' on the 7th with 'half a dozen Majors etc being in to dinner', whilst on the 9th he had to abort an evening mission in D9675 owing to engine trouble; on the 10th he reported 'attack practice' for a 'special stunt' due later in the month.

Swale's rather brief mention of the 'stunt' hid the fact that it was intended as a rehearsal for a set-piece attack on a German aerodrome. The squadron used Wissant air base, south-west of Calais, as the stand-in, and some seventy Camels took part, rendezvousing near Dunkirk where the aircraft formed into two lines of V formations. The warplanes flew side-by-side at 3000 feet heading along the coast some two miles out to sea. On arrival opposite Wissant they dived east towards the airfield and passed over it at around 500 feet. One line of Camels went over the hangars, whilst the others over buildings on the other side, all units returning to their bases overland.

On 11 August Edwin increased his score again. Leading three Camels in D9675 over Roulers at 9.30 a.m. his formation 'got 3 Huns cold' over the town at 12,000 feet. He picked out the leader, a Fokker DVII with a big white 'T' painted on its left-hand top plane. Closing to point-blank range Swale loosed off some 150 rounds, seeing his tracer rake the hapless German from end to end. The stricken warplane rolled over and plummeted down to strike the ground just west of Roulers, a demise witnessed by Lieutenant Whitlock. It was Swale's eighth confirmed victim. In the afternoon he led five Camels escorting bombers to Courtrai, an uneventful mission with no enemy scouts in sight.

Edwin had a less than pleasant day on 12 August as he took part in a mid-morning patrol over the Dixmude-Ostend area. According to his flight leader, Captain Eric Crundall, Swale developed engine trouble in D9675 and turned away for home at 10.40 a.m. whilst flying at 17,000 feet. Five unfamiliar-looking aeroplanes appeared above him as he headed for base, and he later commented, 'I could hardly believe my eyes, they were monoplanes.' As they approached in formation they appeared to the Derbyshire aviator as 'short straight lines in the sky with large dots in their centres'. One of these unusual adversaries peeled off in a dive to investigate him and Edwin was forced to take evasive action, appreciating that he was still some miles over enemy lines. He was gradually forced down to 5000 feet by the stranger until he reached the trenches just north of Dixmude. At this point the enemy machines mercifully turned away. 'They had it all over me,' confessed a rueful Swale, who was later 'chaffed a good deal about what he said he had seen and was told he must put more water in his drink in future'. His flight leader Crundall later wrote, 'This is the first occasion on which monoplanes have been seen for a long time. In fact I have never seen one all the time I have been on the Continent during this war.' Indeed, they were very much a *rara avis* on the Western Front as, apart from the Fokker E-types of 1915, the only enemy monoplanes besides the E-V to take to the skies were the Junkers CL and D species, which appeared in small numbers in later 1918.

Air HQ were most interested in his report on the incident, and in the evening sent an intelligence officer to question him. He was told that his foe was a new type of Fokker, an advanced E-V parasol monoplane, which fortunately was only supplied in small numbers to the *Jagdstaffeln* in the late summer of 1918. This was probably the first time the new scouts had appeared over the operational area, perhaps from the German air base at Varssenaere, home of Marine Feld *Jasta* 11 where some had just arrived to join the DVIIs stationed there, but within a short time wing failures in the air caused their withdrawal from combat. After modifications they re-entered service as the Fokker DVIII, but too late to have any influence on the course of the war. Swale had enjoyed a lucky escape.

The following day 210 Squadron participated in the 'special stunt', a rare set-piece attack aimed specifically at an enemy airfield, in this case Varssenaere, just south-west of Bruges and north-east of Jabbeke, where the main German fighter and bomber strength in the area was concentrated. The objective was to destroy enemy aircraft on the ground and hit the hangars (one of which housed Gotha bombers used in air raids on England) and fuel and ammunition dumps. The attack force consisted of ten bomb-carrying Camels from 210 (four others failed to make it to the target), each carrying two high explosive and two incendiary Coopers, led by Swale, which formed a starboard column, plus sixteen Camels from 213 Squadron flying to port. Eighteen further Camels from 214 Squadron formed an escort to the two columns, with the American 17th Aero Camel Squadron following the two bombing formations into the assault.

The formidable swarm of over fifty Camels took off and swung out to sea where they rendezvoused off Dunkirk in semi-darkness at 2500 feet, two miles out from the coast. The unseen shoal came in over land from the north-west in a long shallow dive over Zeebrugge, and hit the unsuspecting Germans at around 1500 feet in a simultaneous assault just as dawn was breaking. The half-asleep enemy occupiers of the port must have been totally nonplussed as the massed warplanes came snarling overhead in the half-light, creating the most monstrous racket. Swale's column attacked the airfield hangars and parked aircraft, dropping their loads and peeling away to the right to avoid the Camels hammering the other side of the aerodrome. The pilots were then free to take on any targets of opportunity which presented themselves.

The assault was a complete surprise to the enemy who 'were caught with their pants down' with pilots sitting in their fighters ready for early morning take-off, and mechanics casually standing around whilst the motors were being run up. Edwin commented, 'It was great to see the machines all lined up with engines ticking over and the mechanics running.' The row of Fokkers were enthusiastically strafed, many bursting into flames, and no fewer than four German flyers were killed in the attack, one apparently burned to death in his cockpit. The somewhat laconic official report stated that the strike force 'dropped 36 20lb Cooper and 6 40lb Phosphorous bombs and fired 9,200 rounds on aerodrome, A.A. batteries and men in trenches.'

Swale himself dived to 200 feet to shoot up the base, reporting five enemy aircraft set on fire and a fuel and ammunition dump blowing up in smoke and flames in spectacular fashion. As he pulled away from his strafing run in D9675, his Bentley rotary began spluttering unevenly, 'making very disturbing noises'. He throttled back, turning towards the Allied lines and nursing his faltering machine steadily home. Back at base the motor was stripped down and a bullet strike was found to have neatly drilled through one of the induction pipes. That afternoon Captain Patey found occasion to fly over the smashed-up enemy base, duly reporting 'two groups of burnt machines, one group on each side of Varssenaere aerodrome. One side of the chateau nearby was blackened and burned.' A German report later stated that twelve aircraft of MFJ 11 were destroyed, and another five damaged. The base was so thoroughly hit that it was not used again until 25 November when 202 Squadron RAF landed their DH9s there after the Armistice.

14 August was rather more peaceful after the heroics of the previous day, though Edwin had to return early to base with more engine

trouble. That afternoon he was a pall bearer at a military funeral in nearby Dunkirk. Next afternoon, leading a patrol at 11,000 feet in D9675, immediately south-east of Bruges, five Fokker scouts were seen below his formation. Swale picked out a gaily bedizened fighter, resplendent in green and fawn warpaint, with a yellow tail and black crosses over white circles. He saw most of his 150 tracers hitting the scout at 100 yards' range, and his opponent began falling away in a series of stall turns. The DVII fluttered down and attempted a landing in a convenient field just south-east of Bruges, ending up by crashing headlong into a thick hedgerow. Its demise was observed by two squadron flyers, and destruction was duly confirmed. Later that day Captain Patey force-landed at St Pol, and Swale was sent to pick him up in the evening, returning to base at midnight. On the 16th an afternoon escort to DH9s on a photo reconnaissance mission to Roulers-Bruges-Ostend had the Camels airborne for over two hours 'which didn't half tire us'.

On 17 August a further escort, this time at dawn, to DH9 photo reconnaissance aircraft over Zeebrugge, took Swale's flight as far as the Dutch border, struggling against a 'very strong wind against us' whilst a further escort on the morning of the 19th in thick cloud meant 'that at one time we must have been over Holland'. Two days later, flying D3357, he returned with a malfunctioning engine, which cut out over the airfield and forced him into a motorless landing, due to a rocker arm shearing and damaging the engine cowling. On another later bomber escort in D9675, Swale felt the formation 'must have crossed the Dutch frontier coming back'. The weather turned extremely hot and the squadron had a good deal of trouble with overheating engines.

On 22 August, after a morning bomber escort during which the Dutch border was once again violated, Swale led the whole squadron in an evening sortie for the first time, after Captain Patey 'washed out' with engine trouble. In a mid-morning sortie over Dixmude-Nieuport on the 23rd, having separated from his flight, he carried out a lone attack on seven enemy scouts, but did not succeed in picking off any of them. He came home early the following afternoon with another faltering motor, but was later 'complimented by the C.O. on the work I had done since my leave and he said I should probably get A Flight very shortly.' Swale was obviously regarded by this time as a well-seasoned and reliable veteran, one of the backbones of the squadron. On 25 August Edwin was again complaining about the 'Archie which is getting very bad', though poor weather curtailed flying activities until the end of the month when he took over 'A' Flight as promised, and was recommended for a captaincy. On the 28th there was a celebratory dinner for two squadron pilots, Patey and Joseph, who had both received the Distinguished Flying Cross.

By early September enemy anti-aircraft fire was becoming more and more of a problem. The Germans had sited batteries very close to the front lines and British aircraft were being subjected to accurate and intense 'Archie' from a very early stage in each patrol, often from the time they took off. No.210 Squadron's sector of the line was held by the Belgian Army and the RAF asked Belgian HQ to spot the enemy ack-ack positions when their aeroplanes flew over the trenches and use their own batteries to bombard the Germans with counter fire and force their artillery to pull back. Since the Belgians occupied a quiet part of the line (much of the area in front of their trenches was flooded) they refused the request, intimating they wished things to remain peaceful. A few days later Belgian troops were using a rifle range situated on sand dunes near Dunkirk when a lone Sopwith Camel hove into view and, to the Belgians' chagrin, proceeded to dive down and shoot their inoffensive targets to pieces! Hopefully, the Belgian military authorities took the point!

Edwin took charge of 'A' Flight on the last day of August, and was recommended for a captaincy. 'My word' the 19-year-old confided to his diary. 'I hope I can only prove fit enough for the job.' On 1 September he led a late afternoon prowl in E4406 on the Ypres–Roulers line at 17,000 feet when seven Fokker biplanes appeared below just east of the ruined town. He dived on the rearmost, catching up with it at 8000 feet and firing 100 rounds into it as he closed to some fifty yards. The hostile aircraft went down out-of-control, side-slipping and stalling as it fell to earth, a demise confirmed by Lieutenant Boulton. He might have added to his tally but as he lined up another quarry his twin-Vickers jammed and he pulled away in frustration as the rest of the enemy gaggle broke away and escaped. He was the only member of the formation to actually open fire.

Two days later Swale completed two 'shows' ending in a 5.30 p.m. attack on six enemy aircraft at 8000 feet over Roulers in E4406. He fell on the rearmost DVII which was painted all-over green, expending over 350 rounds as he closed on his target from 100 down to thirty yards. Edwin followed his victim down to 4000 feet as it nose-dived to destruction, impacting near Courtrai in a plume of smoke and flame, a demise confirmed by Lieutenant Pinau. It was the Derbyshire pilot's eleventh victim. 'Some scrap' he noted in his diary, reporting that two further hostiles had been shot down in the combat.

No.210 Squadron were based at Eringhem for a considerable time, and got to know the locality well. The pilots often explored the surrounding countryside on foot, obtained meals in the local estaminets, and enjoyed hot baths in convenient guest houses. They knew a French family in the nearby village very well, perhaps due to their two pretty daughters, one of whom was engaged to a British officer. Some of the squadron flyers were invited over for convivial evenings with their hosts and were treated to light refreshments with them. The British aviators got into the habit of overflying the village on their return from patrols, and indulged in buzzing the house until the girls ran out to wave to them. On one occasion Swale came in too low in his haste to greet the family, and only a last-second wrench on the controls of his Camel allowed him to swerve away and avoid a church spire, which suddenly loomed up in his path. The manoeuvre 'saved me from taking the cross off the top, and myself into the ground'.

On 5 September Edwin took part in a tea-time bomber escort led by Captain Patey whose flight, operating at a lower height than Swale's who were protecting the DH9s, dived on seven enemy warplanes east of Roulers. The Camels followed the German scouts, who hailed from *Jasta* 56, down to 1000 feet over Courtrai, and though one hostile was reported crashed, the flight leader and Lieutenant Yerex, a New Zealander of American parentage who later founded a Central American airline, failed to return. Both men were reported missing, but thankfully survived as prisoners of war. Edwin bemoaned the fact that he had to remain 'up top' leading the rest of the formation.

Captain Herbert Patey, twenty days short of his 20th birthday at the time of his capture, probably due to engine trouble, was a good friend of Edwin's. A Londoner, he was tall and well built, 'always in the thick of any horse-play and binges' and was regarded as a good flight leader, 'a dashing, attack-on-sight type'. His Camel, B7280, which Edwin had once flown, was evaluated by the Germans and was later put on display in Berlin. Now fully restored, it is part of the collection of the Polish Aviation Museum in Cracow. With no fewer than eleven German victories to its credit, B7280 may well be one of the most distinguished World War One combat exhibits still extant. Sadly, Patey only survived the end of the war by a few months, dying in London in the great influenza pandemic in February 1919. Later that day Elisabeth, Queen of the Belgians and Prince Alexander of Teck were the distinguished guests of the unit. 'She shook hands with us all and spoke to us' he confided to his diary. 'She was jolly nice and her children too.' The visit ended with a photo session.

The following day, after a lunchtime fleet patrol that took the unit's Camels some twenty to twenty-five miles out to sea off Ostend, Swale led his flight in an evening line sweep in E4406 at 11,000 feet. Near Ostend he sighted five Fokker DVIIs beneath him, and led his formation down in a dive. He concentrated on the rear biplane, which boasted a black-and-white striped tail, aiming 250 rounds from his twin Vickers at between 100 and 50 yards as he closed with his prey. The Fokker dived away with Edwin in close pursuit, and he followed it down to 6000 feet, seeing it plunge into the ground some half-mile east of the port. Confirmation of the victory was again provided by Lieutenant Pineau who secured a second out-of-control claim. Edwin's 'kill' may have been FlugzgMech Hans Howe, killed in action with *Marine Feld Jasta* 111 on that day.

The Swale premises in Vicar Lane, Chesterfield, established by Edwin's father Arthur early in the 20th century.

A youthful Edwin Swale poses in his naval uniform after commissioning in the RNAS at the age of 19. (*Margaret Howard*)

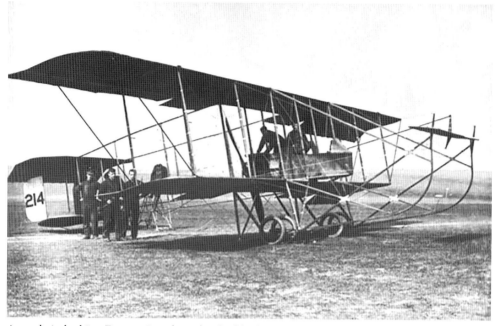

An archaic-looking Farman Longhorn 'pusher' biplane of the type in which Edwin undertook his *ab initio* training. The name derived from the frontal protrusions which carried one of the elevators.

The famous Sopwith Camel scout – 'skittish but formidable' – which was flown with expert ease by Edwin Swale over the Western Front in 1918. The artist has exercised licence with the warplane's serial number as B920 was actually carried by an Avro 504A!

A line-up of 10 RNAS Squadron Sopwith Camels taken before the unit became 210 Squadron RAF on 1 April 1918. The aircraft belong to 'A' Flight and are striped in red and white. Even the wheels are embellished in a variety of designs.

A Camel of 'C' Flight, gaily bedizened in blue and white striping. This example was flown by Captain L. Coombes, a 15-victory ace.

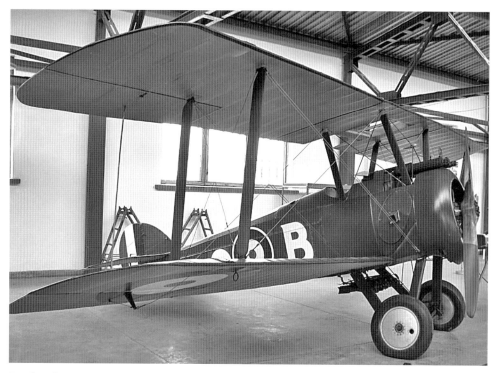

Displayed in Cracow Museum, beautifully restored Camel B7280 was flown by Edwin in August 1918. The scout features dark green colouration in contrast to other preserved Camels which are painted dark brown. (*Helen Maley*)

Edwin's charismatic commander in 210 Squadron was Australian Major B. C. Bell, DSO, DSC with whom he struck up an unlikely friendship.

A drawing of Edwin's 'A' Flight Camel D3332 on patrol in October 1918. The red, black and yellow tail and wing streamers denote his status as flight commander. (*Margaret Howard*)

The bulk of Edwin's victories were scored against the redoubtable Fokker DVII like this example in Munich's Deutsches Museum. The aeroplane was acknowledged as the best German fighter in service over the Western Front in 1918.

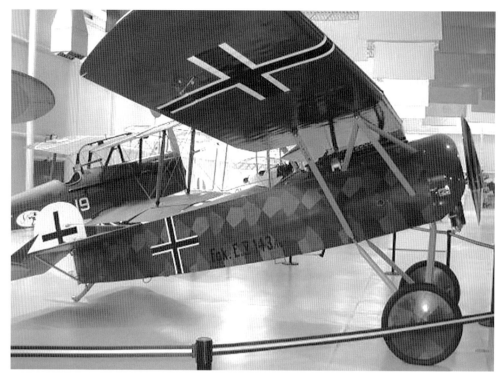

Edwin may have been the first RAF pilot to meet the Fokker E-V in combat in August 1918. Wing flutter caused its withdrawal from service, but it reappeared in October as the DVIII, too late to influence the air war. This example can be seen in the National Museum of Naval Aviation in Florida. (*Tommy Ware*)

A Fokker E-V on the left, with a DVIII in the distance, pictured on Varssenaere airfield in August 1918, shortly before the RAF attack on the 13th of the month.

Captain Herbert Patey DFC, an 11-victory ace with 210, was a friend of Edwin's, and was captured on 5 September 1918 when his Camel B7280 (picture 6) was shot down in combat. (*Norman Franks*)

Another friend was Captain Harold Mellings DFC, DSC, a 15-victory ace who was killed in action on 22 July 1918. (*Norman Franks*)

'C' flight Camels line-up at St Marie Cappelle in the summer of 1918. F5914 is the nearest machine, followed by B7183. The warplanes carry the white ball insignia but all traces of the showy 10 RNAS paintwork have long since disappeared, replaced by a more prosaic green. (*N. Franks*)

Captain Clement Payton DFC, seen here in his earlier role as an observer, claimed 11 victories with 210 before he was shot down by enemy ground fire on 2 October 1918. Edwin recorded 'the bastard Huns got him with a flame projector'. (*D. Hambleton*)

Edwin's elder brother Duncan served with the Sherwood Foresters (Notts and Derby) Regiment, and was killed on the Western Front on 5 October 1918, just over a month before the war's end. (*Helen Maley*)

Duncan, only 21 at the time of his death, is buried in the Commonwealth War Cemetery at Doingt in Picardy. (*CWGC*)

By October 1918 Edwin was a captain leading 'A' Flight. This portrait shows him wearing the early-type DFC ribbon with a silver rosette indicating a bar to the decoration. His rank is shown by the bars on either side of his cap badge. (*Margaret Howard*)

This full-length image shows Edwin in full uniform, a hybrid type of dress before standardisation of colour, rank badges and styling following the war. (*Norman Franks*)

Hady House, Spital, Chesterfield, was the Swale family home from 1913. A house was built in the grounds in the 1920s for Edwin and his new wife. (*Helen Maley*)

An aerial view of the Camphill Gliding Club, Great Hucklow, Derbyshire, founded by the Derbyshire and Lancashire Gliding Club in the 1930s. Edwin and his family flew here at weekends both before and after the Second World War. (*Martin Simons*)

Another view of the Camphill glider field taken at ground level during one of the National Championships. (*Martin Simons*)

Decorated with the Nazi swastika, this Schlempp-Hirth Minimoa glider was exhibited at Camphill in 1938, towed by the Klemm monoplane seen in the distance. The famous woman pilot Hanna Reitsch visited the club and met the Swale family. (*Martin Simons*)

Looking more the bookish Intelligence Officer he became, rather than a highly-successful fighter ace, Edwin poses as a pilot officer in October 1939 on rejoining the RAF. (*Margaret Howard*)

Newly-commissioned Edwin with his wife Dorothy at Hady House in the autumn of 1939. Does the 40-year-old pilot officer exhibit relief at relinquishing the boredom of civilian life for the excitement of military service? (*Richard Rudin*)

Edwin's son Duncan pictured as an aircrew cadet in 1941, shortly before his departure for America. (*Richard Rudin*)

Edwin left the RAF as a wing commander overseeing Ultra code-breaking intelligence, during which he collected no less than three Mentions in Despatches. (*Richard Rudin*)

Accompanied by daughter Margaret who sits in the cockpit of an Olympia 1 'Blue John' sailplane, Edwin surveys the scene during the International Gliding Competition at Camphill in 1949. (*Helen Maley*)

After passing out as a pilot in the USA Duncan spent several frustrating months in Alabama as an instructor, piloting the North American Harvard AT-6 trainer like the American example shown here, flown by another Derbyshire aviator, Michael Mycroft.

Duncan emerged as a highly successful intruder pilot with 107 Squadron, and was awarded both the British and American DFC. (*Helen Maley*)

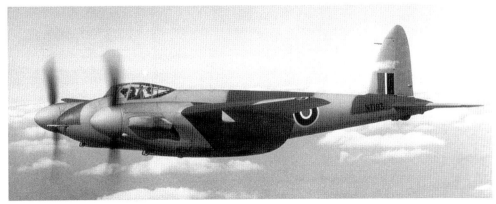

Duncan flew the superb de Havilland Mosquito VI with its formidable nose armament and useful bomb load on many night incursions over enemy territory.

Edwin relaxes in the garden of Hady House with the family dog around 1960, by which time he was a well-respected member of Chesterfield Borough Council. (*Helen Maley*)

Pictured at Hady House circa 1959 this image shows the extended Swale family. Back row l-r: Edwin, wife Dorothy, daughter Margaret, son Duncan. Middle row: son-in-law Derek Rudin with son Richard, Arthur's wife Ruth, father Arthur, mother-in-law Sarah, Edwin's daughter-in-law Joan with son Andrew. Front row: grandson Philip Rudin, and grandchildren Diana, Helen and Robin Swale. (*Richard Rudin*)

On 8 September Edwin recorded 'the splendid news that I have been awarded the D.F.C. I only want my Captaincy to come through now.' The citation for the award described him as:

> A successful and skilful pilot who has destroyed three enemy machines and one kite balloon, and has, in addition, driven down four aeroplanes out of control. On the 15th of August he attacked one of five Fokker biplanes; this machine was driven down out of control and, on attempting to land, crashed.

Swale's promotion to captain was duly gazetted on the 12th. 'By Jove, I am lucky,' he confided to his diary. It was certainly not luck that played a part in his advancement, but solid professionalism, skill and leadership ability. He possessed all the attributes of a successful fighter ace, including an offensive spirit, and the ability to shoot straight at close quarters, picking off usually unsuspecting enemy with one or two fatal bursts. He had rarely been under the guns of an adversary and few Spandau bullets had ever struck his machine. As one of the undoubted stalwarts of 210 Squadron his advancement was both timely and well deserved.

The middle days of September were quiet, with bad weather hampering offensive operations, the only exceptions being a familiarization flight on the 9th showing a new pilot the lines, and a bomber escort on the 13th. With poor weather supervening he took himself off to St Malo on the 15th to view a sports event, an enjoyable visit, although he 'was thinking of Home rather too much'. On an early morning foray to Ostend on the 16th he noted 'three large fires burning to the south' of the port, and later that day, piloting his usual E4406, he made an early return with a malfunctioning engine. Unfortunately, the day was marred by the reported loss of two of the squadron's flyers, Captain Lewis and Lieutenant Marquick.

On the 17th of the month Swale had his closest brush with death since joining his unit. No.210 Squadron had embarked on a series of high offensive sweeps, flying up to 20,000 feet and above, in open cockpits, with no oxygen and inadequate protective clothing. The dangers of constant high flying without oxygen were perhaps not appreciated at the time, but several World War One aeronauts later commented on the symptoms that a lack of oxygen may have produced on some pilots, leading to poor landings and other pieces of defective flying. One 210 pilot later wrote, 'My sight is not as good as it used to be and now long after the war I think I must have been suffering from eye strain due to lack of oxygen on very high flights.' At 5.15 p.m. Edwin's flight of five aircraft were over Ostend at 19,000 feet. Suddenly, enemy scouts were sighted above them as the British warplanes skimmed along the top of a thick cloud bank. Edwin's fellow pilots spotted the diving adversaries and manoeuvred to avoid their attack.

At that precise moment a random German anti-aircraft shell exploded directly underneath his Camel, E4406, tearing holes in the wings and tail unit, severing two control wires, and giving both pilot and fighter 'a good shaking up'. In fact, Swale thought his stricken machine was going to fall apart. His wingman, Lieutenant Sanderson, saw what had happened and as his leader slowly descended, unwilling to put any further stress on his airframe, he turned to engage the enemy and protect his number one. The other four members of Edwin's flight succeeded in keeping the *Jasta* pilots off his neck, but Sanderson was wounded in the ensuing dogfight. Swale was thankfully swallowed up in cloud at 17,000 feet, but once inside the safety of the murk he found he could only turn his fighter in one direction, and curved round as slowly as possible for home, fearing that any increase in speed would cause his badly damaged machine to disintegrate.

Swale descended a considerable distance under cover of the cloud blanket, eventually breaking clear at 1500 feet, directly and unhappily over the enemy-held port of Ostend. He veered towards Dunkirk, using the coastline to guide him and proceeding home at the slowest pace, afraid to open up his Bentley motor. He was forced to fly in a straight and level direction, and though the German flak gunners threw up a barrage they were unable to nail his faltering Camel despite its predictable flight path. Fortunately, no enemy scouts put in an appearance, and the twenty-minute return to the Allied lines proceeded without undue alarm, apart from the unusually inaccurate German ack-ack. He eventually sighted his old base at Tetegham, just outside Dunkirk, and then the home of 204 Camel Squadron. As he thankfully sank into a landing E4406 gently hit the ground, and the shrapnel-pocked wings literally collapsed on either side of his cockpit with a rending crunch and the twanging of parting wires. It had been a miraculous escape, and a mightily relieved Edwin, whose flying skill had brought him safely home, was grateful for two days off ops, enjoying some rough shooting with the CO on the 19th. He subsequently wrote, 'I was back safe, unharmed and lived to fight another day.' During his return flight he had 'no recollection of anything passing through my mind except that I was stringing a whole lot of curses together'.

Edwin's adventures were by no means over. He wrote that a few days later he went aloft in F3107 and 'the first anti-aircraft shell which came up when we were over the lines burst about a mile away and I just wanted to run for it.' In fact, his engine seized up and he only just managed to reach home base. He later confided that:

> Just for the moment I could not face it, and I came back after that patrol and had a chat with my C.O. (Major Bell) who was quite an understanding man, although a bluff character in his way. He said, 'well that won't be very good for you will it Swale now that you are moving up to Flight Commander.' I said no. 'Well what shall we do about it?'

Edwin revealed that, 'In those days you had to settle things for yourself and I said "leave it to me sir, I will go over the lines and see what I can do about it."' Bell told Edwin it was up to him, and as the latter recalled:

> I took an aircraft, went on my own, and I knew where I could get plenty of anti-aircraft fire with a possibility of not being spotted too quickly ... I flew at only a moderate height, anti-aircraft shells came over, in fact it was so close that I could actually smell the smoke from the bursting shells and I simply set my teeth very rigidly and flew straight on, taking no evasive action for several minutes in the midst of this fire, then turned round and came back and my nerves were cured. From that time on anti-aircraft fire did not affect me at all. I just shrugged it off.

After the loss of E4406 Edwin piloted F3107 on an early line patrol, but 'had to turn back owing to engine seizing and only just got in the Drome'. Later in the day he 'Went to Wissant for a new bus', enjoying a good lunch and returning in D3332, the aircraft he flew for most of his remaining time with the squadron. In the evening he visited his wounded flight member Lieutenant Sanderson, borrowing the CO's car for transport. Next day a morning flight was aborted due to 'the dickens of a wind' but he later enjoyed another 'good drive' in the CO's motor. Little aerial activity took place until the 24th when the squadron tangled with some sixteen Fokker biplanes at 13,000 feet on the Dixmude-Nieuport patrol line. Piloting his new mount, Edwin took part in a whirling dogfight during which he attacked the *Jasta* leader, loosing off some 100 rounds at fifty yards, seeing his tracer hit home as his opponent stalled away in a series of side-slips, which ended in the inevitable impact south of St Pierre Cappelle. 'Some scrap,' he confided to his diary, 'the Huns are evidently waking up on this front.' 210 claimed four 'kills', though Lieutenant Joseph suffered a slight wound in the engagement.

On the evening of 26 September Edwin was entertained to dinner in the mess of 204 Squadron, stationed at Tetegham, whilst on the following day his flight were returning from an afternoon sweep when Lieutenant Light had to force-land near Furnes due to enemy ack-ack fire. Edwin circled the downed scout to check that the pilot was safe and the machine relatively undamaged. On reporting to the CO he was asked if he could locate the aircraft and pilot, taking a trailer and crew. He replied in the affirmative and was ordered to bring them both back if possible. Unfortunately, the Germans had a heavy artillery piece located in the Ostend area, which they occasionally used to hot things up around Dunkirk. The 27th was one of those days, and Swale's route took his rescue party into the vicinity of the shelling. The missiles were falling every ten minutes or so, but one round had exploded near a Chinese labour camp whose occupants had decided to decamp *en masse*. Their panicking numbers seriously impeded Swale's progress and it was near nightfall when he was challenged by a Belgian sentry. Edwin's halting French was no help, and the exasperated sentinel eventually replied in perfect English, 'If you will speak in English I will understand you better.' Edwin soon found out that Light was safe but injured, and the aircraft could not be retrieved until daylight. He had to return to base with his mission unaccomplished. That night he confided to his diary, 'The push starts tomorrow. May I come through it safely.'

The 'push' in question was one of a series of co-ordinated Allied offensives that between the end of September and the Armistice pushed German forces back to the River Scheldt. It was the third in a succession of assaults, and concentrated on the Ypres battlefront in Flanders, with the British Second Army co-operating with the Belgians and French. On the left flank the Belgian Army aimed to clear the enemy from the Houthulst Forest, whilst the British, attacking to the right on a sixteen-mile front between Ypres and Armentières, advanced some six miles on the opening day of the assault. Frustratingly, torrential rain on succeeding days slowed down progress and the operation was closed down on 2 October. Further south the British Fourth Army launched their own attack on the 29th, breaking through the St Quentin Canal defences of the Hindenburg Line.

On the 28th the major British offensive 'push' led to the squadron's scouts once more carrying bombs, which were deposited on railway lines and locomotives at Lichtervelde junction in the Torhout vicinity, Edwin scoring a direct hit on a train and helping to shoot up ground targets. On a second sortie his oil pipe severed, seizing up the motor and necessitating an early return home. At teatime a third raid was thwarted by numbers of enemy warplanes who prevented the squadron from dropping their Coopers at an effective height. They had to loose them at 1000 feet, sacrificing the necessary accuracy. The unit dropped some two tons of bombs on various targets during the day, downing two opposing aircraft for no cost, and he subsequently wrote that, 'All objectives were taken – a good day's work.'

Next day, flying F3116, on an early morning patrol on the Roulers–Torhout–Dixmude line, Edwin spotted some fifteen Fokker DVIIs prowling below in the Staden locality. He picked out his victim, diving onto one of the *schwarme* and aiming 100 accurate rounds into the single-seater from fifty yards down to point-blank range. His target careered vertically away under his fire, rolling over onto its back at 1000 feet, spinning down to smash into the ground near Courtemark in a rising plume of smoke and flame, its destruction witnessed by Lieutenant Pomeroy. On the last day of the month he recorded the capitulation of Bulgaria in his diary with the comment 'The beginning of the end for certain.'

The first day of October saw Swale doing 'three shows with no time to myself at all'. Around 9 a.m. he had an indecisive combat with fifteen German scouts over Houthulst Forest, west of Roulers, where the Belgians were attacking the German front, whilst Lichtervelde railway junction underwent further bombing around lunchtime, with direct hits scored on the station and lines, and several fires started. At 4.40 p.m. Torhout junction and nearby Roulers suffered further bomb hits before 210's Camels and some eleven Fokker DVIIs met over the latter town. In a turbulent engagement, which began at 11,000 feet, Swale latched onto a dark green biplane leading the enemy formation, which he hit with a 100-round burst of tracer at the point-blank range of thirty yards. The badly hit warplane tumbled down, hitting *terra firma* south-east of Roulers, its destruction confirmed by Lieutenant Giles. Edwin immediately found himself behind a second Fokker, also painted dark green and with a broad white band round its fuselage. He glued himself to the German fighter's tail, firing over 200 rounds into it from less than 100 yards, following his adversary down to 2000 feet as it stalled, side-slipped and rolled away out-of-control. He was unable to witness its inevitable end as other enemy aircraft were still circling above. The squadron claimed six 'kills' in this lively combat and the delighted Swale later wrote 'I led every show and we were successful all through', though he confessed to the loss of two squadron pilots, including a Major Sibley.

The following day opened with a 7 a.m. low-level bombing attack on Cottemarck Railway Station, which took several direct hits and was left ablaze. Sometime after 10 a.m. the squadron mixed it with a gaggle of Fokker biplanes and Triplanes over Roulers in a series of swift-moving but indecisive combats, but Captain Clement Payton was hit by ack-ack and went down on fire to his death. For once Edwin let his emotions get the better of him as he confided to his diary, 'The bastard Huns got him with a flame projector.' He himself 'had a good old scrap with a Triplane but only drove him down'. On the 3rd a teatime flight over the lines revealed 'Nothing to report except fires in

Ostend as a result of fleet shelling.' He reported, 'Jenkins is missing tonight. By jove I hope he turns up alright.' The absent Canadian Captain Stanley Jenkins, though injured, did in fact eventually return safely to the unit. Edwin visited him in the field hospital on the 7th 'and had a good chat with him'.

Engine trouble enforced an early return to base on the 4th, whilst the 5th was quiet, though Edwin was not to know that on this unhappy day his brother Duncan was killed in action at the age of 21. He spent the afternoon and evening in Calais, and the following day went on a rough shoot, one of several he enjoyed in the company of the CO with whom he had established something of a rapport, but 'the birds were too shy so we didn't get any'. These more peaceful pursuits doubtless helped the hardworking aviators to preserve some kind of normality.

Edwin Swale made his last combat claim around 8.20 a.m. on the morning of 8 October. He reported a 'big scrap' in his diary when 210 clashed with a mixed formation of enemy warplanes four miles north-east of Roulers. In a twisting skirmish in D3332 at 11,000 feet with eleven Fokkers, he plunged on the rearmost machine, which boasted a white tail and letters on the fuselage. He got off 100 rounds from his twin Vickers at fifty yards' range, seeing his tracer strike home; the stricken DVII went down in a steepening dive, streaming a thin trail of smoke, to crash and burst into flames, a demise witnessed by Lieutenants Hughes and Boulton. It is often difficult to be certain of victims' identities in speedy clashes such as this, but his prey may well have been Flg Kurt Oertel of *Jasta* 20, shot down in combat near Roulers on that day. Eight more Fokkers came down from above, and, though two were shot down, Lieutenants Pinau and Hopper were both posted missing after the combat, though the former, an

American, survived a forced landing and was taken prisoner. Edwin's victory was his seventeenth, all despatched in a period of just over four months in front-line combat. It is significant that no fewer than fourteen of his kills were scored against the redoubtable Fokker DVII, pride of the German fighter fleet, which was considered so dangerous an opponent that the subsequent peace treaty specifically mentioned the ultimate disposal of these machines. Unusually, not a single enemy two-seater fell to his guns, quite a remarkable occurrence.

That evening Swale enjoyed dinner with his CO and members of 217 Bomber Squadron at their base at Crochte. On the 11th came the dreaded tidings concerning his brother. 'Got the awful news from home', he confided to his diary, 'that Duncan has been killed in Action. I can hardly believe it yet. What is life going to be like now?' The following day he wrote, 'Haven't got over the news about Duncan yet and have been feeling pretty rotten all day. The C.O. is sending me back to H.E. (Home Establishment) so I pray that I shan't have to do any more flying before I go.' Swale had been given the facts concerning Duncan's death. His brother was serving with the 6th attached 11th Battalion of the Sherwood Foresters at Doingt, a small village on the eastern outskirts of Peronne, which was captured by the 5th Australian Division on 5 October. Duncan was coming out of the lines at the time, and as his troops passed through the rear support trenches they stopped to bivouac and a long-range German shell fell amongst the group, killing him instantly. The saddest irony was that Edwin was preparing to visit him by kind permission of his bluff CO, Major Bell, who had his own private car and driver, and had arranged for him to use the vehicle for the journey. His agony of mind is recorded in his diary entry for the 13th when he wrote, 'When am I going to get home. I am worrying about it greatly and the War tonight and again tomorrow.' Duncan was interred in the Doingt Communal Cemetery Extension in Picardy, maintained by the Commonwealth War Graves Commission, where he still lies.

Edwin had almost reached the end of his front-line combat stint. He helped escort a low-level bombing attack on the 14th at 5 a.m., followed by two more 'stunts' later that day, recording good results, though Lieutenants Whitlock and Fountain went missing. He dropped his last bombs over Roulers, and his final brush with the German Air Service occurred at 1.20 p.m. on that same busy date when he led an assault on four enemy scouts east of that much-hit town, followed by three others east of Thorout, but was unable to make any claims. He recorded in his diary that, 'The war started again … we are making some quite good advances and we worked hard all day.' 'Awful' weather the following day meant no flying, but Edwin enjoyed a spin to Dunkirk in Major Bell's car for the statutory bath and tea.

Swale's last operational flight was in his faithful D3332 on 17 October around 11 a.m. when a patrol over Ostend revealed that the Germans seemed to have abandoned the port. To check this was correct, Edwin and his companion actually landed their Camels on the beach just outside the town and were able to confirm that the enemy were in full retreat from Belgium. The news was passed to HQ and steps were taken to bring King Albert of the Belgians back to his own country. In his logbook Edwin recorded a final aggregate of just over 440 combat hours in the air over the trenches, and some 500 in total.

Edwin Swale was posted to Home Establishment on 21 October and later the same month was awarded a well-deserved bar to his DFC. The citation described him as:

> A gallant and determined officer. On 1 October Captain Swale led his patrol to attack eleven Fokker biplanes; in the engagement that ensued he drove down the leader, which crashed, and caused a second machine to fall out of control. In addition to the foregoing, this officer has destroyed nine hostile planes and driven down five out of control.

For much of the autumn he had been Senior Flight Commander and later revealed that out of an establishment of eighteen pilots over a period of less than eight months, 210 had lost fifty-three of its flyers, either killed, wounded, missing, rested or prisoners of war. By November 1918 the squadron had claimed 345 victories, with 29 pilots achieving ace status, but with 105 casualties it had been the hardest-hit British scout unit of the war.

Swale spent his last few months in the air force at 42 Training Depot Station (TDS) at Hounslow, a base for single-seat fighter tutelage, commencing in late November. Here he enjoyed short practice flights, air tests, cross-countries, formation exercises and air-to-ground firing in the RAF's latest fighter, the Sopwith Snipe, successor to the famous Camel. He left Hounslow in mid-February 1919 and was demobilized shortly afterwards.

The loss of his brother was a life-changing event in Edwin's life. One of his squadron comrades was an American who had enlisted by travelling to Canada. Swale, whose daughter revealed that he enjoyed a natural aptitude for mechanics and gadgets of all kinds, and a notable skill in driving early vehicles and motor bikes, became friendly with him and learned he was a motorcycle expert who held US records, and who was taking up a post-war opening as chief distribution manager in North Carolina for Indian Motor Cycles. He had asked Edwin to join him and he had, apparently with Dolly's approval, decided to accept the offer. However, Duncan's death meant that he now had an obligation to replace him in the family business, which is what he duly did.

Chapter 4

Peace and War

After his dangerous and exciting seven months' service with 210 Squadron, Edwin Swale returned home to the realities of a career he had not sought or wanted. He had written that his brother had been 'the real business head', but felt it was his duty to take on his responsibilities and run the family enterprise. He married Dorothy Asquith in 1922, a union that produced a son, Duncan (born 1923), and a daughter, Margaret (born 1927), and the pair moved into a house built for them by Edwin's father, Arthur, in the grounds of Hady House, and named Rhone House. Swale realized that 'the mental effects of my experiences' in the war were working, and though he returned to worship in the Chapel, he 'was certainly not the same person and many questions were going through my mind as to the validity of all that side of my upbringing'. Gradually, his long-held faith began to fade and he became a confirmed agnostic, to the great disappointment of his parents, though they never questioned his decision.

When Swale eventually broke away from the Church, he joined the Adult School Movement:

> and for quite a fair time I spent Sunday mornings going to the Adult Local School which had their own premises in the town and met lively minds on the same quest as my own.

> Minds much more lively than I had met inside the Church, which not only stimulated but solved quite a few of my own problems and tended to formalise the point at which I was arriving from a religious point of view, which in fact moved fairly rapidly on to a complete break from the Church.

Edwin felt that he was simply reverting to his own grandfather Seth's ideas on religious belief, which was 'a genuine personal decision which I had come to not lightly but only after deep thought and consideration'.

The newly married Swales lived in some domestic comfort in their new home, with two live-in servants and a gardener to cater for them. The family business did well in the inter-war years and doubtless provided the wealth to maintain the appropriate standards for an upper middle-class household. Though I have no intention of describing Edwin's long period of public and political service in Chesterfield in any detail, it cannot be totally ignored in this narrative. He joined the Young Liberals in the early 1920s, and was persuaded by a local businessman to become chairman of the town branch of the newly formed League of Nations Union. He spent much time travelling in the area, recruiting members and talking about the aims of the League, in particular its hopes for avoiding future wars, but was soon persuaded that the general public were apathetic, and not inclined to listen.

Edwin was elected to the Chesterfield Borough Council in 1927 as a Liberal, though within twelve months he had defected to the Labour Party, then very much a minority group in council. However, over the course of several years he found that local politics did not provide him with the satisfaction he had anticipated, and that his presence in the Council Chamber was not actually changing anything. Somewhat disillusioned, he indicated in 1933 that he was not available for re-election, and as he wrote, 'Thus ended my initial venture into public life … and in that sense I retired into private life for the period right up to the second world war.'

However, Edwin did find a very satisfactory substitute for politics in a completely different environment. He later wrote of his efforts to 'find an outlet' for his energies, intimating that 'I don't know what I should have done had I not done this.' He was referring to a return to flying. Quite by chance he went to visit a newly established gliding club, the Derbyshire and Lancashire, set up by an amalgamation between enthusiasts from Derby and Manchester, who had joined forces and leased an old farm at Camphill, site of an Iron Age hill fort on a picturesque escarpment known as Bradwell Edge, near the village of Great Hucklow in the heart of the Derbyshire Peak, which enjoyed stunning views and provided the updraughts so necessary for the sailplanes. Swale was enthused by the prospect of actually flying again, and as a former RAF pilot received a wholehearted welcome from the members. He was soon taking a leading part in the development of the club and the field, and in due course became the Senior Flying Instructor. He purchased a caravan, which was kept on site, and was also used for family touring holidays in the summer. Every weekend in the gliding season the Swale family could be found at Camphill, and in due course his wife and children all learned to fly.

Swale's son, Duncan, described as 'flying mad' by his father, became, together with his close friend Godfrey Slater, the youngest qualified glider pilot in the country at the age of 15 when he took his 'C' certificate, and Edwin himself joined a syndicate that purchased a Rhonbuzzard sailplane for the sole use of the three members. He later boasted that 'from the year 1935/6 right to the outbreak of the Second World War I was a leading figure in the gliding world, not only in Derbyshire but abroad as well.' He established a height record of 7000 feet, and the club became so famous it was visited by some of the leading lights of the German gliding movement in 1938.

Among these distinguished visitors was Wolfram Hirth, noted German gliding pioneer and sailplane designer, who had a prototype Schlempp-Hirth Minimoa two-seat glider towed to England by a Klemm monoplane in the hope of selling it. It was exhibited at Camphill in 1938, but was an unpopular design as the view from the rear seat was so poor. Hirth was accompanied by Hanna Reitsch, the equally celebrated test and glider pilot, many of whose records still stand, and who famously landed a Fieseler Fi 156 Storch in Berlin on 26 April 1945 in an attempt to fly Hitler out of the doomed capital. Reitsch was once described by the test pilot Eric 'Winkle' Brown as a 'fanatical aviator, fervent German nationalist and ardent Nazi, but was surprisingly feminine. She was smallish, fair, petite', whilst another Camphill glider pilot called her 'a weird woman but a brilliant pilot'. Edwin's daughter, Margaret, remembered Hirth and Reitsch, the latter described as 'a very small blonde haired lady' passing their caravan as they were cleaning it, and asking if they could look round the trailer. When they left, her mother said, 'What a personality. I would have followed her anywhere.'

Reitsch's death in 1979, with no post-mortem, led some authorities to suggest she had committed suicide, perhaps using a cyanide pill given to her by the Führer himself. Interestingly, when war broke out in 1939, the locals recalled the recent visit of the Germans to Hucklow and perpetrated some low-level acts of vandalism at the farm, including breaking windows and suchlike.

After World War Two, British Pathé made a short film about gliding at Hucklow called *Wings for Pauline* in which his daughter, Margaret, who had inherited her father's gift for flying, played the part of the eponymous Pauline and in which Edwin also enjoyed a role. However, during the later 1930s, Swale revealed that whilst he enjoyed a full personal life with the business, the Gliding Club and the family, he was 'restless and uneasy in my personal life'. He wrote in his autobiography that, 'If this is to be a true reflection of my personal experience then it must of necessity contain some comment of personal mental strains and stresses which occurred between 1935 and 1939.' Salvation eventually came with the outbreak of World War Two.

After the return of Neville Chamberlain from Munich in 1938, Edwin Swale became convinced that 'this was only an interlude and that now there was no hope of avoiding in any way a second world war'. He wrote to the Air Ministry offering his services, mentioning his earlier war record, and the fact that he had been involved in the gliding movement and still kept up his 'interest in the practical as well as theoretical aspects in the flying world', and indicating his willingness to perform any duties the authorities saw fit. The Ministry wrote back explaining that when any emergency arose they would get in touch with him, so he 'patiently waited', and within fourteen days of the declaration of war he received notification to travel to London for an interview for a possible commission in the Royal Air Force Volunteer Reserve.

When Edwin went to London for interview the officer in charge asked him if he recognized him. Swale was surprised when the man revealed that he had been the CO of the Naval Flying Section at Dunkirk in 1918, and had recalled his name from over twenty years previously. The 'interview' turned into a 'chat across the table about old times' and Edwin, asked what he might like to do, suggested that as he had kept his flying practice up, he might serve as an instructor in the rapidly expanding Air Force. His interviewer thought there was a better way of utilizing his expertise and experience, and sent him on his way to await his verdict. A few days later Swale received the welcome news he was to be commissioned as a pilot officer in the RAF. He was to be posted to intelligence work and was to report to No.12 Group headquarters, Fighter Command, at Hucknall, just outside Nottingham. Within a month of war breaking out, Pilot Officer Edwin Swale reported to his new HQ, and prepared for a very different kind of war.

No.12 Group was tasked with the aerial defence of the Midlands, Norfolk, Lincolnshire and North Wales, and was commanded by the contentious Air Vice Marshal Trafford Leigh-Mallory, brother of the late George Mallory of Everest fame. Due to his beliefs, or rather non-belief, Edwin was always exercised as to how to answer questions posed as to his religious denomination, and at Hucknall he persuaded the Group Adjutant to list him as a Rationalist! This problem arose every time he took up a new appointment. On one occasion an adjutant asked him to interview representatives of the three main Christian faiths, Church of England, Roman Catholic and Nonconformist;

Swale was more than amused that an 'unbeliever' should be briefing Church representatives on their rights and duties in connection with their service flocks! Another time the AOC of one station scheduled Edwin for a Church Parade. He had the courage to suggest to the great man that he would take the airmen as far as the church door, but would not venture inside, but wait outside until the end of the service and march them back to their billets. The AOC's reply, delivered 'in a rather jocular vein' was both 'prompt and expressive' (in fact it was 'bugger off'!), but the request was never repeated. In fact, Swale only ever attended two official parades, one when Lord Trenchard came to visit his unit, and once when King George VI attended his HQ in Holland in late 1944.

During that first winter of the so-called 'Phoney War' Swale, using his own private car with a petrol allowance because of the shortage of vehicles, organized a series of visits to Observer Corps posts within the Group, lecturing on aircraft recognition, then a skill still in its infancy. At the time radar cover only extended along the coastline, and inland it was vital that enemy aircraft could be quickly distinguished from those of the RAF. After his 'very useful and interesting winter occupation', which 'went down extraordinarily well and which I do believe gave some excellent results', he was convinced that the local OC 'was very well briefed on aircraft recognition'.

Edwin was then moved down to Fighter Command HQ at Bentley Priory at Stanmore in Middlesex, where he was promoted to the rank of flight lieutenant and worked in the office of Air Chief Marshal Sir Hugh Dowding, Commander-in-Chief Fighter Command, and a man for whom Swale developed a deep respect, and who in his eyes, 'never got the praise or recognition for the work he did as leader during the

Battle of Britain. I shall always respect that man', he wrote, 'for the single-minded purpose which crowned his success.'

When the Battle of Britain commenced, Swale had the chance to observe 'Stuffy' Dowding at close quarters as he had a desk in his office where he assessed and dealt with all incoming information on raids as it filtered through from the nearby Operations Room. It was one of Edwin's duties to keep the C-in-C or his deputy up to speed on any incoming intelligence emanating from all parts of the country. In the Intelligence Office in the underground Control Room at Bentley Priory was a special telephone linked directly to the Prime Minister, Winston Churchill. When the phone rang, 'everybody jumped and took the receiver off with some trepidation.' In the early hours of one morning after 'the biggest and most hectic day of the Battle of Britain' – presumably 15 September – Edwin, who had been on continuous duty over the previous day and night, was still in the office at 7 a.m., and had just gathered together the figures concerning German losses for the press. The PM's phone rang and Swale heard the gruff tones of Churchill on the other end of the line.

Edwin offered to put the Prime Minister onto the senior staff officer, but Churchill replied, 'Never mind doing that, have you been on duty all night?' 'Yes, and all day sir,' was his response. 'Well,' said the great man, 'you know more about it than he does anyway, so you tell me.' Swale thus had the job of giving the information direct to the Prime Minister, and then later had to explain to the SSO what he had done. The latter understood Swale's dilemma and accepted his explanation. 'That was the only time', reminisced Edwin, 'that I remember speaking to Winston Churchill during the war virtually face to face.' He remembered seeing him quite often, especially during the Blitz on London, but did not personally talk to him. 'This was just one of these little memories of a stirring time,' he later wrote, 'which sticks in the mind and always will do.'

After the excitement of the Battle, Swale was not sent back to 12 Group, but was ordered to report to the Air Ministry where he was told that a new group had been formed for the defence of North-West England, the Isle of Man and Northern Ireland. He was duly posted to the Group base at Samlesbury airfield near Preston, Lancashire, as Senior Intelligence Officer, with the rank of squadron leader, of the recently established No.9 Group. Edwin was briefed as to how the base would develop, and was told that his job would be to organize the intelligence side of the undertaking, and he soon became aware that intelligence and operations were completely different.

Swale had not previously been aware that RAF intelligence officers were under the direct control of the Air Ministry and were not responsible to the COs of the stations to which they were posted, except for disciplinary purposes. As he wrote, 'I now had the very difficult task, although a tremendously interesting one, of opening up and developing an Intelligence Service for a completely new group.' As part of his duties, he had to visit a number of other RAF stations within the Group, and he was able to co-ordinate these visits with those carried out by other personnel from other sections who travelled from place to place in the HQ's light communications aircraft allocated to them. In this way Swale was able to build up his flying hours by personally piloting these machines with the permission of the staff officers who accompanied him. One of these individuals would settle down in the cockpit as soon as the aeroplane was airborne and fall asleep after telling Edwin, 'She's all yours – wake me up when we get there.'

When visiting the Isle of Man, Edwin always landed at the main airfield, which was situated at the north end of the island, near the capital, Ramsey, and, in a period of strict rationing, the locality was popular with Swale and other RAF personnel, as the calculation for restricting wartime foodstuffs had been based on the population on the outbreak of war. This had been boosted by holidaymakers visiting at the time, and consequently there was a surplus of many kinds of rationed foods freely available in the shops. Edwin and his passengers took full advantage of this boon, by loading up their aircraft with goods that had long since vanished from mainland stockists. On one occasion his passenger in the aircraft had just visited the Lake District in his car whilst on leave, and suggested they overfly the area so that he could see it from the air. Unfortunately, they took so much time searching the locality that evening was falling as they turned for home. In gathering gloom Edwin could only find his way by heading for the coast and making his way to Samlesbury by following the River Ribble. They touched down on the aerodrome and the motor immediately cut out due to lack of petrol, preventing him from even taxiing to the hangar. On another occasion, whilst flying to Wrexham in bad visibility, Edwin ran into the Liverpool balloon barrage and was lucky not to hit any of the dangling cables.

Swale spent two years 'of very active work' in the North-West, overseeing his subordinate intelligence officers who established a complete network from every station. The Station Commander at Samlesbury never quite appreciated Edwin's autonomy 'and sometimes quite resented it'. However, he evidently did well in this post and when the build-up for the invasion of Europe began, the Air Ministry sent for him again. He was interviewed at the new Allied Intelligence HQ, and, after 'a lot of aimless chat', was shown a map of the Continent and asked where he thought any invasion should take place. Without hesitation Edwin pointed to Normandy and was asked, 'How did you know that?!' He pointed out it was the logical spot for very valid reasons, and explained:

> Firstly, you could make a feint and get all the German armour withdrawn to the North bank of the Seine, and then blow up all the river bridges from the sea to Paris, and while the invasion was taking place you could isolate the battlefield completely from any German armour reinforcements for at least 14 days if not longer, because if all the armour was north of the Seine it could not get across to us without going all the way round to Paris.

Reinforcements could then be harassed from the air all the way and, 'You could have at least 14 days' grace whilst you consolidated your bridgehead before any German armour reappeared.'

Swale's interviewer seemed surprised at Edwin's quite logical conclusions, and revealed that fresh tactics were being evolved for the invasion, including a new Tactical Air Force (the 2nd TAF), part of 84 Group, which would include, fighters, fighter-bombers, and light/medium bombers. These squadrons would work in close co-operation with the invasion forces, and Intelligence HQs would operate within the army groups themselves. He was told that he would be responsible for organizing intelligence for the Canadian

Army and thus become Senior Intelligence Officer (SIO) with the rank of wing commander. This meant starting from scratch again, but with the advantage that he could personally choose his own staff from among officers he knew. The new HQ was initially based at Cowley in Oxford and Swale 'had a tremendously exciting time in building up a completely new unit which had got to be mobile'.

Edwin's new command had to be able to move with the army, at the same speed and with full inter-unit co-operation. He later wrote that, 'It was one of the most interesting periods of the whole of my life.' Before the invasion date, his command moved to the south coast to join the forces assembling at the various airfields where they were given the task of keeping track of the emerging threat from Hitler's 'vengeance' weapons, particularly the Fieseler Fi 103, the so-called V1 (*Vergeltungswaffe*) flying bomb or 'Doodlebug', powered by a pulse-jet and which was the world's first cruise missile. Swale built up a file of every V1 launch site and it was one of his tasks to keep watch on all these bases. When observation suggested that a particular site appeared to be nearing completion, bombing raids were launched on these 'Noball' sites, which eventually delayed the deployment of the V1s until 13 June, a week after D-Day. Edwin felt that the watch his unit kept on the V1 launch pads, and the tactics employed in hitting them, postponed the first firings for over six months.

Swale recalled that one tactic employed by RAF fighters, which could carry a 500lb bomb, was to locate the entrance to each command post, which controlled the launching of the robot aircraft. The entrances were rightly seen as the weak spots in the heavily reinforced concrete structures, and aerial photographs showed they were conveniently marked by pathways leading to the main doors. Where possible,

Spitfires and other fighter-bombers were encouraged to fly on a low approach to the sites, aiming to drop their delayed-action loads just short of the doorways, hoping to cause considerable damage to the posts, or at the least make things very uncomfortable for the launch crews. When Swale's unit landed on the Continent he was able to check on the accuracy of many of the RAF's attacks, and he was also gratified to learn that only one of the many V1 launch platforms had escaped his attention, and this, built into a hollowed-out hillside, was only in the initial phase of construction.

When Swale's command was readying itself to join in the invasion, a special officer from Air Ministry Intelligence visited the unit, and explained to him and other senior officers the top secret details of Ultra, the generic name for intelligence obtained through intercepting and decoding enemy messages via the Enigma project at Bletchley Park. Swale himself was to receive this intelligence personally and would interpret it for his superiors, and not even his second-in-command would be privy to the secrets. Data would reach Edwin in its raw form, and it was his responsibility to pick out what was necessary and useful to him for his own unit's use, and discard the rest. The information came directly to him via an intelligence officer working for the Ultra cryptanalysts; it was always delivered by printed transcript and he had to undertake to destroy anything not of interest to him within twenty-four hours of receiving it.

Writing his autobiography some thirty years after the end of the war, when Ultra was still top secret, Swale had to be necessarily vague about his work. He recorded that he:

was never able to speak freely on this and all I can definitely say is that … it was never possible, with the information which we had, for the Germans to win, because the information was so utter and complete on their movements, not only over Europe but elsewhere, it was not possible for them to win the battle. Beyond that I can never say anything more about the matters which we used and how it was got.

One illustration of the value of breaking the German codes concerned the Luftwaffe Operation *Bodenplatte*, the attack on Allied airfields, which took place on New Year's Day 1945. Edwin received news that the action was to take place on Christmas Day, and when it failed to materialize, his prophecy was treated somewhat sceptically by certain senior officers.

Swale's response was that 'it was coming'. Interestingly, other sources suggest that Allied Intelligence failed to fully detect German intentions regarding the large-scale raid. There were few indications in Ultra transcripts concerning the plan. Some German communiqués suggested an impending ground attack mission, but enemy comments on a 'special undertaking' were not followed up. Likewise, other messages relating to low-level attack practices were ignored. Swale stated that he kept in contact with RAF reconnaissance elements, and when the weather was fit – which wasn't often around Christmas time – he had aircraft reconnoitring the Low Countries to see if anything was happening. On the morning of New Year's Day he received the news that considerable formations of German aircraft were heading towards the Allied lines.

The information was that the enemy warplanes were Messerschmitt 109 and Focke-Wulf 190 single-engined fighters, apparently being led by Junkers 88s and Messerschmitt 110s, who were acting as navigational guides. Swale wrote that he got in touch with the appropriate bases with the news that Luftwaffe fighter-bombers were heading for RAF and USAAF airfields, and any Allied fighters capable of taking to the air (and some airstrips were snow or icebound) were able to intercept and break up the incoming raids. He remembered that at the daily briefing with the CO, an air vice-marshal and several senior officers, he was gazing out of a window in the Dutch Army barracks where the morning conferences were held, when the CO asked him what he had seen. He turned round and said, 'There's a bloody 110 circling over the gateway. He laughed and jumped up but sure enough there was!'

Bodenplatte was an attempt to cripple Allied air forces in the Low Countries to assist Hitler's last great assault against American forces in the West, the so-called Battle of the Bulge, an attempt to drive westward to take the Belgian port of Antwerp. Originally scheduled for 16 December, *Bodenplatte* was repeatedly put back due to poor weather. It finally took place on 1 January 1945 and was the last large-scale strategic offensive operation ever mounted by the German Air Force. The attack on the airfields cost the Allies some 300 aeroplanes, plus some 190 damaged, but most of these were parked on the ground and were replaced within a week. In return Allied fighters and anti-aircraft fire caused losses of 143 enemy pilots killed or missing, with seventy captured and twenty-one wounded. A number of the enemy machines were shot down by their own flak as they crossed German-held territory, whose AA gunners had not received news of the attack. Interestingly enough Edwin's son, Duncan, was awarded a US Distinguished Flying Cross for his part in aerial operations in support of the American army during the battle.

The Luftwaffe never really recovered from this misconceived action, which cost the lives of a number of experienced fighter pilots, flyers the Germans could not afford to lose. Swale's final comment on the exploit was, 'I was very thankful that I had taken the precaution of having a watchdog out to see if anything was happening.' Of the Ultra intercepts he could only write, 'On the background of our intelligence my lips must be sealed on this.' It was several years later that the background to Allied cryptoanalysis was finally revealed. It is reported that when the code-breaking secrets were made known to the world shortly before Edwin's death, he was horrified – as far as he was concerned the secret was expected to go, together with everyone involved, to their graves.

One incident that seems to have soured Edwin to some extent concerned his AOC, who was presumably Air Vice-Marshal Harry Broadhurst who was at the time the youngest AVM in the RAF. Swale wrote that, 'He had only been with us a short time and was comparatively young to carry such an appointment.' One morning, out of courtesy, Edwin showed Broadhurst his daily report to London HQ. 'He queried part of the report,' Swale recorded, 'because it did not reflect too favourably on his actions and asked if I couldn't alter the report.' When Edwin refused the request the AOC 'was very upset' and the former ruefully reflected, 'It probably cost me one of the OBEs which were later given out.' However, he did have the distinction of no fewer than three Mentions in Despatches.

Chapter 5

'Like Father …'

Edwin's son, Duncan, born in April 1923, was educated, like his father, at Chesterfield Grammar School, and from an early age shared his father's love of aviation. Keen to follow him into the air, he commenced gliding instruction at Camphill in December 1937. By the following April he was judged competent enough to take his 'A' test, followed rapidly by his 'B' test in May and his 'C' in June. His glider log shows that both the latter were 'very well flown' and that he was considered a more than competent pilot by the age of fifteen, at the time the youngest qualified sailplane flyer in the country. He took part in the 1939 National Gliding Competitions at Camphill in July of that year, but was airsick several times in the rough, windy conditions prevailing that month. By the outbreak of World War Two he had completed forty hours in the air; after leaving school he worked in the family business for a year, and as soon as he reached the age of 18 he volunteered for the RAF.

After his initial 'square bashing' Duncan was sent to America for pilot training by the United States Army Air Corps, under the so-called 'Arnold Scheme', named after the US General of that name. He ended up at Tuscaloosa, Alabama, at the SE Air Corps Training Centre in December 1941, just after Pearl Harbor and America's entry into the war. The unit operated Stearman PT 17 biplanes, and his first *ab initio* (or Primary in US terms) flight took place on 20 December.

He soloed on 6 January 1942 as an acting pilot officer u/t and moved on to his Basic training at Gunter Field in late February. He remained at Gunter until the end of April, flying the more advanced Vultee BT 13, a low-wing Harvard lookalike with a fixed undercarriage.

Duncan's final Advanced instruction took place at Craig Field, Selma, Alabama, from 30 April until 3 July, when he was awarded his RAF 'wings'. Here the training was on the state-of-the-art North American AT-6A Harvard monoplane, which boasted such refinements as a retractable undercarriage, flaps, and a variable-pitch airscrew. His only hairy moment was a crash-landing on 11 May, but his progress as an aviator was obviously regarded as so marked that he was appointed a flying instructor at Craig, and remained in Alabama until April 1943.

Whether this was to his liking or not is not recorded, but for the next ten months he bumbled around the skies with rookie trainees in Harvards, plus the occasional trip in a Piper Cub or Aeronca L-3C. On rare occasions he was able to handle a modern warplane, usually a Curtiss P40B or C Tomahawk, indeed his final flight in America on 30 April 1943 was in such a machine, but by this time he must have been positively aching to get into the action on the other side of the Atlantic. He had the not inconsiderable number of 872 flying hours in his log by then, and his final assessment by his American superior was, 'Excellent all-round pilot. Good pursuit material. Should do very good on fighters.' In US terms 'excellent' was second only to 'superior' in flying terms, and was doubtless much appreciated by the Derbyshire aviator.

Duncan's wish for active service was granted and by late July he was back in England, at No.7 Personnel Reception Centre (PRC) in Harrogate, North Yorkshire, practising on the Link trainer. On 1 September, by now a flying officer, he reported to No.12 Air Fighting Unit (AFU) at Grantham, Lincolnshire, where he retrained on twin-motor aeroplanes including the Avro Anson and the obsolescent Bristol Blenheim I and IV. Whether this pleased him or not is again a matter of conjecture, as he would doubtless have preferred to follow his father as a fighter pilot (or 'pursuit' in US terms), but he signed off at Grantham on 11 November with an 'above average' assessment and 911 hours in the air. A few days earlier he had found time in his busy life to marry his fiancée, Joan Elizabeth Dean. The pair had met when he was 17 and had corresponded when he was in America – in fact, he had proposed by letter when he was stationed there. They were married on 5 November, their anniversary invariably celebrated with a bonfire party!

On 5 January 1944 Duncan was posted to 60 Operational Training Unit (OTU) (Night Intruder) at High Ercall, near Shrewsbury in Shropshire. Here he tested himself on the twin-Merlin de Havilland Mosquito III fighter-bomber, teaming up with Dutch Sergeant (later pilot officer) Van Der Helstraete as his navigator. The superb Mosquito, one of the great RAF successes of the war, served in many capacities, and Duncan's role was to be that of low-level night operator, interdicting enemy road, rail and air communications, deploying up to four 500lb general purpose bombs, and a formidable nose armament of four 20mm cannon and four .303 machine guns. Flying at zero feet over Occupied Europe, these aircraft caused havoc to German movements and Duncan speedily tackled night flying, gunnery, bombing, and much low-level activity. By the end of the course, on 28 March, his assessments were: as a fighter-bomber pilot above average; in bombing skills a good average, and in aerial gunnery above average.

At the beginning of April Duncan and his navigator were posted to 107 Squadron, stationed at Lasham in Hampshire. Originally formed in 1917, the unit was revived in August 1936 as a bomber squadron equipped with Hawker Hinds. It subsequently graduated to Bristol Blenheim Is and IVs, then Douglas Boston IIIs before re-equipment with de Havilland Mosquito VIs in February 1944. Swale's first action took place on Mayday when, piloting Mosquito OM-D, he attacked Juvincourt airfield, depositing four 500lb bombs whilst facing light flak in the process. It was the first of many night intruder operations for the pair, commencing with a series of raids on Luftwaffe airfields, flying low and gunning targets of opportunity whilst hedge-hopping in both directions. By the end of April he had completed over 1000 hours of powered flying.

With the onset of D-Day on 6 June attacks intensified, with particular emphasis on road convoys, rail links and rolling stock, with 107's aircrew hitting lorries and trains whenever they were sighted. Duncan's 500-pounders certainly made more impact than the relatively tiny 20lb Coopers his father's overburdened Camel had dispensed! His heavy schedule of night operations added fuel dumps and road and rail bridges to the target list, using flares to illuminate likely targets. Railways became important objectives in early July, including trains and tunnels; on the 11th Duncan's bombs breached a railway bridge at Elbeuf, whilst on 2 August a rare squadron attack in daylight devastated a chateau at Chatelleraut, obviously a target of some importance. Operations were usually routine, but a mission on the 12th on a rail line between Falaise and Argentan went awry when Duncan's bomb load hung up and he was forced to return with the missiles on board, no doubt carrying out a rather more-than-careful landing!

Night-time road and rail patrols continued into September, with offensives against river traffic and marshalling yards. In advance of the Arnhem airborne assault Dutch targets were added to the list. On the 17th the unit hit a barracks in Arnhem itself in another daylight mission, during which Duncan's Mosquito was holed by light flak in two places. The pair's first tour ended two days later, with an 'above average' assessment for his piloting, though dropping to 'average' only in bombing and gunnery'! By this date he had recorded 1175 operational hours in his logbook.

After a short rest Swale and Helstraete volunteered for a second tour of duty and returned to 107 Squadron on 27 October. The unit had moved to Hartford Bridge in Hampshire, and their operational tasks continued much as previously, with low-level nocturnal attacks throughout November, including the successful targeting of locomotives with 500-pounders and cannon. On the 19th of the month the squadron moved to Epinoy/Cambrai in France, and from 22 December their Mosquitoes began missions in support of US ground forces involved in the so-called Battle of the Bulge, hammering ground transport in the Ardennes region. Somewhat ironically, in view of Duncan's father's involvement in Operation *Bodenplatte*, his Mosquito, HX165, was destroyed on the ground at Ursel airfield in Belgium by marauding Focke-Wulf 190s in a dawn raid on New Year's Day 1945!

Attacks on German road and rail transport, together with pinpointed army strongpoints, carried on without respite throughout January with bombs and cannon, though one interesting trial on the 29th involved a daylight dropping of captured enemy anti-personnel 'butterfly bombs' on St Croix airfield, which was only a short distance from the British Gold Beach in Normandy. There was sad news for the extended family that month when Edwin's young cousin Kenneth Swale, a 21-year-old flying officer navigator with 139 (Pathfinder) Squadron, was killed when his Mosquito XX KB263 (XP-D) crashed in very poor weather when returning to Thurleigh airfield in Bedfordshire after a mission to Berlin on the night of 14/15 January. Both Kenneth, who had been decorated with the DFC, and his pilot, Flight Lieutenant Peter Drane DFC, died in the accident. Kenneth, who had worked for the family firm and who had survived forty-five operational flights on Avro Lancasters, had only recently converted to Mosquitoes; he was buried at Boythorpe Cemetery in his native Chesterfield.

Rail wagons were the main quarry in early February, with assaults on marshalling yards at Dillenburg and elsewhere. Duncan's busy second tour ended on 9 March 1945, and Flight Lieutenant Swale finished his wartime career with 1265 flying hours logged and another 'above average' proficiency rating. He was awarded a Distinguished Flying Cross in December 1944, plus a US DFC, the latter presumably for his work during the Ardennes operations, though his time as an instructor in America may have helped his cause. The citation read:

> Flight Lieutenant Swale has completed 60 operations
> as a Mosquito intruder pilot. He has gained the award

for gallantry and devotion to duty in the execution of air operations, and has obtained some fine results on operations by night. In June last year he bombed a railway siding, starting a large fire and on other sorties he has attacked transport vehicles, trains and barges. Despite adverse weather he has invariably persevered with his tasks and has always shown great determination and a fine fighting spirit.

Father-and-son DFCs are not that common, especially among pilots serving in two separate World Wars, and Duncan's success must have delighted his father, Edwin.

Duncan was posted to 13 OTU at Finmere in Buckinghamshire on 7 April as a flying instructor, piloting mainly Mosquito IIIs, though he did get his hands on a Supermarine Spitfire VC on 1 July, plus sundry less powerful machines during a protracted, and doubtless boring few months, during which he celebrated the end of the war in Europe. At the end of November he was sent to No.7 Flying Instructors' School at Lulsgate Bottom near Bristol to take a course on tutoring, though he might have had some right to bemusement as he had enjoyed – if that is the right word – more than one spell of teaching recruits to fly. The unit deployed Airspeed Oxfords, not aircraft calculated to warm the heart of a former Mosquito night intruder pilot! The only excitement occurred on 7 December when his instructor pulled the wrong lever and collapsed the undercarriage when the Oxford he was in was firmly planted on the ground! He ended the course on 14 January 1946 with the usual 'above average' flying rating, but a Category 'C' as a flying instructor, the latter with a logbook note 'to apply for a recat as soon as possible' by the unit wing commander, though it would seem he never did.

Duncan's final posting was on 28 January when he reported to 13 OTU Middleton St George Conversion Squadron in County Durham, where he ended his service career tutoring on Mosquito IIIs, a consistent diet of which he endured until his last flight on 28 June, landing on that day with just under 1500 flying hours in his log. He did a little sailplane flying with the local gliding club to keep his hand in during this time, and was demobilized on 9 July. He did no further flying until he joined the Royal Air Force Volunteer Reserve as a flying officer and took to the air intermittently with No.9 Reserve Flying School (RFS) at Doncaster, from January 1949, piloting humble de Havilland Tiger Moths, a far cry from the speedy and powerful Mosquitoes from the same stable he had once handled so expertly.

In early June 1951 Duncan, as a member of the RAFVR, was called-up for a three-month refresher flying course at 6 FTS at Ternhill in Shropshire. Here, he flew Harvard trainers until mid-July when he graduated to a Supermarine Spitfire 16 – basically a Mark IX with a blister hood, pointed tail and an American-built Packard Merlin 266 engine. On 9 August he had his first flight in a jet aircraft as a passenger in a two-seat Gloster Meteor Mk.7 in preparation for conversion to the type. On 13 August he moved to 2 Squadron 103 Flying Refresher School (FRS) at Full Sutton near York where, for the first time, he had a taste of actual jet flying when he piloted a twin-boom de Havilland Vampire I in an extensive series of flights which lasted until the end of the month and involved some fifteen hours in the air, taking his flying hours to 1659.

In early September 1952 Duncan, by now a flight lieutenant, reported to No.208 Advanced Flying School (AFS) at Merryfield in Somerset for a fifteen-day spell of continuous flying (known as 'Booster Training'), which mixed pupillage in a dual Meteor 7 and more single-seat practice in a Vampire I, entailing a full range of high speed runs, climbs, aerobatics and formation exercises. He signed off with an 'average' rating as a 'jet jockey.' Duncan's final flight with the RAFVR was a thirty-minute stint at Doncaster in late July 1953 in a de Havilland Chipmunk trainer, which was considerably slower than the fast jets he had piloted the previous September! He concluded his part-time service career with 1671 hours in the air, by which time he had flown over twenty aircraft types. He gained his private pilot's licence after the war and his last flight in a powered aeroplane was in a Taylorcraft Auster in a ten-minute solo at Exeter Flying Club in March 1962. However, Duncan retained his love of gliding, and between 1955 and 1959 he piloted sailplanes at Camphill, mainly in the Olympia 1 'Blue John' Glider. His final flight took place in August 1959, a seventy-minute feast of loops and formation exercises, and he signed off with some seventy-seven hours of powerless aeronautics to his name.

After the war Duncan returned to the family business though his heart was always in flying, and he had been offered a permanent commission in the post-war RAF. However, his interests lay elsewhere and when it eventually became obvious that neither of his sons were keen on working in the undertaking it was sold in the late 1970s. Duncan undertook other jobs for a while, but sadly developed a brain tumour and died in August 1981 at the early age of 58, a grievous loss to his wife and family.

Chapter 6

A Busy Life

Edwin's job of Senior Intelligence Officer finished with the ending of the war. He handed over his duties to the Disarmament Commission, though he remained in Germany for some time, whilst he awaited demobilization. One of the problems he encountered concerned the RAF fighter squadrons which remained with the occupation forces. Operational flying had, of course, ended, and though the pilots could keep in practice to some extent, there was little else to do and a number of bored young men sought an outlet for the lack of aerial activity. Quite by chance Edwin discovered the site of an old Luftwaffe gliding school in the Hartz Mountains which had been used by the Germans since the 1930s. Here was an opportunity for the pilots to relieve their frustrations, and Swale received permission to revive the undertaking.

Swale recalled that a unit of the RAF Regiment had been attached to his command for protection, particularly against the sometimes lawless bands of foreign ex-forced labourers who were all attempting to get home, and who were often in need of food and shelter in the chaotic conditions of post-war Germany. Edwin set about to bring the old glider club into existence again, manning it with airmen from two nearby squadrons. His hope was that the flyers would become interested in operating engineless aeroplanes, which would help to keep them in practice and relieve their tedium. He located a number of gliders once operated by the school, some of which had been stored for safekeeping in nearby salt mines. He also found one of the original craftsmen in a nearby village, and procured him a workshop with the appropriate furnishings and fittings. Some of the gliders needed repairs, and Edwin heard of a store in Hamburg, which contained a large supply of aviation three-ply wood. A lorry was sent to pick up a load of the material, which would be used to renovate the more dilapidated machines, and prepare them for flying.

Edwin also did a trade-off with the local Burgomaster, who was more than a little afraid of the roving groups of foreign ex-conscripts who had little love for their former masters. In exchange for supplies of butter, milk, eggs and other foodstuffs, which helped to augment his forces' more basic rations, he agreed that his RAF Regimental unit would provide protection to the inhabitants of the surrounding area, and the troops actually marched through the local settlements in a show of strength to assure them they would be safeguarded. 'So,' wrote Edwin, 'we got on very good terms with the locals, and had good supplies of fresh food to complement our own supplies.'

The day arrived for the first glider launch, 'a tricky one,' as Edwin acknowledged, 'because I was dealing with people who had never handled a glider, and had never seen one launched.' There was no mechanical means of launching the sailplane which had been dragged to the top of a hill and which had thus to be propelled by the old 'bungee' method of using elastic ropes and plenty of muscle power to drag it off the eminence. Swale was the obvious choice for pilot, though he acknowledged he had not flown a glider since before the war and the operation thus contained some little danger. It was also an aircraft unfamiliar to him, and he had no idea of its flying characteristics. He had to shout his orders for take-off from the cockpit for the ground crew to launch him, and he was duly shot off the top of the hill and successfully flew the strange beast, gradually soaring to over 800 feet, and giving all the spectators a thrill in the process.

Edwin had to land the machine at the foot of the hill as there was no landing ground on the hilltop, and the glider had to be manhandled uphill again. The flight was Swale's first solo after the war, and he believed it was also the first post-war civilian sailplane launch in Germany. The RAF pilots were all eager to try out the craft, and, by the time he had left to be demobilized, the glider school had become a flourishing enterprise. He believed that RAF personnel stationed in the area kept it going for some years after he had gone. As he wrote, 'So I completed the war, as you might say, almost as I started it, by gliding.'

One of Swale's first post-war tasks was to place the family business on an even keel. His wife had shouldered the main responsibility for running it during the war, owing to the serious illness of his father, and despite her efforts it had of necessity lost ground due to wartime shortages. As previously stated, it was not my intention to dwell on his civic contributions to his native town, but some record must be made of his achievements in this sphere as they resulted in the awards of the OBE (1958) and CBE (1964), and the granting of the Freedom of the Borough to him in 1966. Shortly after his return from military service Edwin was made a Justice of the Peace, and, in June 1946, was elected to the Council. He duly became an alderman and mayor like his father before him.

Swale wrote of these times that, 'life was full of activity, tremendously full … on the public front as well as the private.' Over the next twenty-five years he served the Borough Council continuously, appearing on most Council Committees and officiating as chairman of several of the most important ones, including the Finance and Education Committees. A local secondary school was named after him in honour of his work in the latter sphere, but like others in the Borough, lost its appellation after reorganization in 1990. He was also a member of the Derbyshire County Council for twelve years, and represented both Councils on the committees of other bodies and organizations. His membership of the Association of Municipal Corporations (AMC) meant periodic visits to Strasbourg, and when he became chairman of that body he was placed on the Executive Committee of the International Union of Local Authorities, and under their auspices attended overseas conferences in such diverse localities as Brussels, Berlin, Washington DC, Stockholm and Belgrade.

As a representative for the British Council, Edwin went to several conferences held under their auspices. In 1953 he was elected Mayor of Chesterfield after standing to oppose someone parachuted in by a pressure group to take up the position. Swale had 'never agreed with the principle that length of service on the Council should itself imply a right to become Mayor' and had therefore allowed his own name to be put forward in contention. His action led to his religious beliefs being challenged when a Nonconformist Minister found out about his atheism and declared he was not a fit person to be made mayor in view of his non-religious convictions. Swale retorted that as mayor he would put aside all political and religious affiliations during the period of his mayorality, and any further protests quickly fizzled out. As mayor he was invited to Westminster Abbey for the Queen's Coronation, and retained a 'lasting memory which will remain with me to the end of my life'. Swale was also active in fostering the idea of twin-towns, and, during his lifetime, Darmstadt in Germany and Troyes in France became twinned with the Derbyshire town. Of his admission as an Honorary Freeman of the Borough, the eulogy contained the words 'by his wise counsel, particularly in the field of education and youth work, he has been unstinting in his promotion of the development of the Borough and its people.'

Much of the other information on Edwin Swale's municipal service with the Council and other bodies is of necessity rather tedious and of little general interest. Sadly, in the late 1960s, he suffered several bouts of ill health and this, coupled with certain disputes within the Labour group in Council, led him to determine to retire gradually from public life. His deadline had been on achieving the age of 70, but he did in fact linger on for a few more months. He generously stated that, 'Whatever I achieved, however small it may be, it could not have been achieved without the constant and uncomplaining support of the woman I married.'

Towards the end of his autobiography Edwin Swale wrote:

> Whether it will interest anybody I do not know, but I honestly believe and always have done, that every individual owes something to the community which has made it possible for him to enjoy a reasonably good life, and should try to pay some of that debt back during his or her lifetime.

Edwin Swale need have no doubt that in war and peace he did just that, first as a fearless fighter ace in the skies over the Western Front, climbing into his Sopwith Camel to patrol Dixmude-Roulers-Bruges-Ostend in his open-cockpit wood-and-canvas biplane, with no protective armour, parachute or oxygen supply, whilst facing a determined and courageous foe, then as an intelligence officer burdened with the weighty secrets of Ultra and Enigma, and finally as a dedicated servant of Chesterfield Borough Council and an acknowledged expert in the field of lighter-than-air flying, he did much more than his share in fulfilling the stated aims of his life. Many men have been knighted for less.

Edwin Swale, noted son of Chesterfield, died in July 1978 and was buried in Spital Cemetery, not far from the family home at Hady House. The final sentence of his life story contained the statement that:

> if I had my life again I would still try to pay back to society some of the things that society made available to me which otherwise I could not have had ... if you live by a philosophy like that, I do not think you will go very far astray.

Few people could wish a better epitaph.

Appendix

Combat Claims – Captain Edwin Swale
DFC and Bar

All claims with 210 Squadron RAF.

Date	Aircraft Flown	Locality	Type	Claim
30.5.18	Camel D3392	W Armentières	Pfalz DIII	Destroyed
5.6.18	Camel D3392	Estaires	Kite balloon	Destroyed
17.6.18	Camel D9613	SE Zillebeke Lake	Albatros DV	Destroyed
20.7.18	Camel D9613	SE Ostend	Fokker DVII	OOC
		SE Ostend	Fokker DVII	OOC
22.7.18	Camel D9613	S Ostend	Fokker DVII	Destroyed
1.8.18	Camel D9675	N Lille	Fokker DVII	OOC
11.8.18	Camel D9675	W Roulers	Fokker DVII	Destroyed
15.8.18	Camel D9675	SE Bruges	Fokker DVII	Destroyed
1.9.18	Camel E4406	E Ypres	Fokker DVII	OOC
3.9.18	Camel E4406	Courtrai	Fokker DVII	Destroyed
3.9.18	Camel E4406	Courtrai	Fokker DVII	Destroyed
6.9.18	Camel E4406	W Ostend	Fokker DVII	Destroyed
24.9.18	Camel D3332	S St Pierre Cappelle	Fokker DVII	Destroyed
29.9.18	Camel F3116	Courtemarck	Fokker DVII	Destroyed
1.10.18	Camel D3332	SE Roulers	Fokker DVII	Destroyed
		E Roulers	Fokker DVII	OOC
8.10.18	Camel D3332	NE Roulers	Fokker DVII	Destroyed

Sources

Edwin Swale Autobiography (typescript circa 1970).

Edwin Swale Pilot's Logbook 1918.

Edwin Swale Diary 1918.

Duncan Swale Logbook (1941–53).

Franks, N. and Guest, C. *Above the Trenches Shores*, (Grub Street 1990).

Crundall, E. *Fighter Pilot on the Western Front* (William Kimber 1975).

Index